BONSAI
and PENJING

AMBASSADORS OF PEACE & BEAUTY

From the Collection of the
National Bonsai & Penjing Museum
U.S. National Arboretum
Washington, D.C.

Including excerpts from *The Bonsai Saga, How the Bicentennial
Collection Came to America* by Dr. John L. Creech

Ann McClellan

TUTTLE Publishing

Tokyo | Rutland, Vermont | Singapore

Published by Tuttle Publishing, an imprint of Periplus Editions (HK) Ltd

www.tuttlepublishing.com

Copyright © 2024 Ann McClellan

ISBN: 978-0-8048-5784-0 PB
ISBN: 978-0-8048-4701-8 HC (LCCN 2016022278)

Distributed by

North America, Latin America & Europe
Tuttle Publishing
364 Innovation Drive, North Clarendon, VT 05759-9436 U.S.A.
Tel: 1 (802) 773-8930; Fax: 1 (802) 773-6993
info@tuttlepublishing.com; www.tuttlepublishing.com

Asia Pacific
Berkeley Books Pte. Ltd.
3 Kallang Sector #04-01, Singapore 349278
Tel: (65) 6741-2178; Fax: (65) 6741-2179
inquiries@periplus.com.sg; www.tuttlepublishing.com

26 25 24   10 9 8 7 6 5 4 3 2 1

Printed in China   2410CM

TUTTLE PUBLISHING® is a registered trademark of Tuttle Publishing, a division of Periplus Editions (HK) Ltd.

Page 1 Japanese Red Pine (*Pinus densiflora*) from the Imperial Household, Japan, 1976.

Pages 2–3 California Juniper (*Juniperus californica*).

Left Japanese Wisteria (*Wisteria floribunda*).

Right American Beech (*Fagus grandifolia*).

Far right Moon Gate entrance to the Chinese Collection.

contents

Left In training since 1625, this Japanese White Pine (*Pinus parviflora* 'Miyajima') survived the Hiroshima bombing and is the oldest bonsai in the National Bonsai & Penjing Museum.

CHAPTER ONE

CHAPTER TWO

CHAPTER THREE

CHAPTER FOUR

CHAPTER FIVE

CHAPTER SIX

CHAPTER SEVEN

THE BONSAI SAGA

FOREWORD

The U.S. National Arboretum, where science meets beauty, is proud to be the home of the National Bonsai & Penjing Museum, the world's first public museum dedicated to the horticultural arts of bonsai and penjing. Founded in 1976 with a gift from Japan to the United States in honor of its Bicentennial, the National Bonsai & Penjing Museum is a focal collection within the U.S. National Arboretum.

Established in 1927, the National Arboretum is itself a living museum and research center. More than half a million visitors visit the grounds annually, where they enjoy the beauty of our 16,000 varieties of plants, the balance of our cultivated gardens and natural landscapes, and the quiet of our 446 acres only a few miles from the U.S Capitol Building.

What they may not know is that they are visiting one of the world's leading horticultural science institutions with collections that include a large and invaluable inventory of germplasm and herbarium specimens to support research by scientists worldwide. In the United States, the National Arboretum is credited with introducing more than 650 cultivars of woody and herbaceous plants into the country. As an entity within the Agricultural Research Service of the U.S. Department of Agriculture, the National Arboretum continues to develop new cultivars and new approaches to detecting and treating plant diseases, ultimately benefitting people in the U.S. and around the globe.

The National Arboretum salutes our National Bonsai & Penjing Museum on the occasion of its 40th anniversary. We applaud the commitment and skill of all those who have made possible the museum's masterpieces of horticultural artistry.

Dr. Richard T. Olsen
Director, U.S. National Arboretum

National Bonsai &
Penjing Museum

PREFACE

In honor of the National Bonsai & Penjing Museum's 40th anniversary, the National Bonsai Foundation is pleased to present the story of how the museum came to be, highlighting some of its treasured trees and viewing stones along with some of the people involved. We hope this book— like the museum itself—will refresh your spirit now and inspire future generations.

The National Bonsai Foundation is a nonprofit organization established in 1982 to sustain the National Bonsai & Penjing Museum and support the museum's mission "to be an international center where superior bonsai and related arts are displayed and studied for the education and delight of visitors." The National Bonsai Foundation cooperates with the U.S. National Arboretum, providing financial assistance and advice, in a private/public collaboration that makes the museum's displays and educational programs possible, fostering intercultural friendship and understanding.

The story of how the Japanese trees, accompanied by several notable viewing stones, came to Washington is a fascinating example of the power of beauty, vision and perseverance. It is well told by the late Dr. John L. Creech, former director of the U.S. National Arboretum and the key proponent behind the gift. Major excerpts of his work, *The Bonsai Saga, How the Bicentennial Collection Came to America*, are included in this book as a tribute to him and to all those whose efforts made possible that extraordinary gift and the museum we enjoy today.

For me, bonsai, penjing and viewing stones are reflections of our souls, bringing nature close to each of us in a unique way. I hope *Bonsai and Penjing, Ambassadors of Peace & Beauty* will serve to enhance your enjoyment of these living and evolving art forms.

Felix B. Laughlin, President
National Bonsai Foundation

Left A Japanese White Pine (*Pinus parviflora*), the same variety of tree used for many bonsai and penjing, is also popular in Japanese gardens. This tree greets visitors at the museum's entrance.

chapter one

A National Collection of Living Arts

Left A Japanese White Pine (*Pinus parviflora* 'Miyajima') from Japan, a Garden Juniper (*Juniperus procumbens* 'Nana') from America, and a Cork-bark Pine (*Pinus thunbergii* Corticosa Group) from China represent the museum's major collections.

Opposite *Koinobori* or carp kites celebrate Children's Day on May 5th in Japan, but at the museum they delight visitors all summer long.

When the National Bonsai & Penjing Museum at the U.S. National Arboretum in Washington, D.C. first opened its doors in July 1976, it was the first public museum in the world devoted to the display of bonsai and penjing. With collections representative of the Chinese art of penjing and the Japanese art of bonsai, as well as an evolving North American collection, it is the most comprehensive museum in the world for the display of the natural beauty in trees writ small. The collections are wide-ranging, including some trees that have been handed down from one generation to another, spanning centuries. Even trees that are not old in years are fashioned to look as though they have been aged by time. It is this combination of small and old-appearing that fascinates the imagination, attracting visitors from all over the globe to come and stand in awe before a little landscape in a pot.

Each tree in the collections is a work of art and has a story to tell. It is these stories that add a deeper dimension to a viewer's experience of each tree. Each was created by one artist, some of whom are legendary. These artists share the skill and eye to work with the small trees, creating works of art that capture the essence of nature's beauty and offering viewers a different way to perceive the mystery of life itself.

In addition to highlighting several of the collections' masterpieces, this book explores the global trends, especially the West's fascination with all things Asian, which culminated in the creation of the National Bonsai & Penjing Museum. It also explores the roles bonsai and penjing have played in the highest levels of international diplomacy as ambassadors of beauty and peace.

The small trees' role as ambassadors began centuries ago when the Chinese art form called *penjing* was embraced and enhanced by the Japanese, along with other Chinese arts like calligraphy. In Japan, the art form was called *bonsai* (pronounced bone-sigh), which means "tray planting." Bonsai now has come to refer to all diminutive trees and plantings in containers no matter what their origins are. Historically and today, the goal of both art forms is to distill and evoke nature's magnificence and grandeur into distinctive miniature living trees or compositions.

To become a bonsai or penjing, a tree or plant with a woody stem is chosen for its natural characteristics and for its potential form. Its roots are trimmed to reduce its size and its branches are cut and wired to grow into the desired shape. Most bonsai and penjing artists have an ultimate view of the tree in mind, which they enhance with specially chosen trays or pots, the same way other artists choose frames to set off their work. The process of the tree growing into the artist's intended shape can take years or decades or even centuries.

CHINA

Ancient China was a highly cultured, complex civilization with a myriad of different aesthetic expressions, ranging from scroll painting to architecture, and it included penjing. In the late seventeenth and into the eighteenth centuries, foreign interest in Chinese arts and goods reached a peak. It led to a fashion trend called *chinoiserie*, fueled by European and North American colonists'

demand for Chinese tea, silks and decorated porcelain. The fervor for all things Chinese included Chinese-style pavilions and pagodas, which were added to gardens.

After centuries of limiting commerce, the Chinese began to promote trade by participating in world's fairs in the nineteenth century, such as the 1876 Centennial International Exhibition in Philadelphia and the 1915 Panama-Pacific World Exposition in San Francisco. War in the world and China's own internal turbulence prevented them from exhibiting again until the 1982 Knoxville World Expo. After President Richard M. Nixon visited China in 1972,

Chinese Gardens in North America after 1980	
1981	Astor Chinese Garden Court, Metropolitan Museum of Art, New York City, New York
1986	Dr. Sun Yat-Sen Classical Chinese Garden, Vancouver, British Columbia, Canada
1990	Montréal Botanical Garden, Montréal, Québec, Canada
1996	The Margaret Grigg Nanjing Friendship Garden, Missouri Botanical Garden, St. Louis, Missouri
1999	Chinese Scholar's Garden, Snug Harbor Cultural Center, Staten Island, New York
2000	LanSu Chinese Garden, Portland, Oregon
2008	The Huntington, San Marino, California

Above A Chinese blue and white hand-painted porcelain dish from 1790–1840, 4.13 x 25.08 x 20 cm, exemplifies the idealized landscapes of the East popular in the West at that time.

Above right A 19th century Japanese woodcut print, *American merchant delighted with miniature cherry tree*, 35 x 23 cm, shows a man admiring a bonsai, possibly thinking of his wife.

there was renewed interest in Chinese arts in the United States, including public Chinese gardens. Interestingly, Chinese gardens were created in Canada at the same time.

The Chinese art form of penjing—the art of creating miniature landscapes on trays, sometimes with plants alone, sometimes with rocks and plants, or other times with rocks only—may have played a role in China's presentations at the world's fairs. Where it surely had an impact at an earlier time, however, was in Japan.

JAPAN

Over centuries, many elements of Chinese civilization migrated eastward to Japan, ranging from the concept of a pictographic alphabet to the tea ceremony. Typically, the Japanese would embrace a Chinese model, then refine it over time to suit their own culture's aesthetic sensibilities. Some say this trend reached an apex of expression with the importation of Zen Buddhism in Japan in the fourteenth century, crystalizing during the following centuries into forms familiar to us today. The

Chinese art form of penjing is a paradigm of this trend. Penjing arrived in Japan with other Chinese arts, then evolved into the more highly codified geometric and controlled art form of Japanese bonsai.

Also following the Chinese pattern, Japan became the new source of Asian inspiration after its opening to expanded foreign trade by Commodore Matthew C. Perry in 1854. Called *japonisme*, this infatuation in the West with Japanese style and design, especially lacquerware, textiles and woodblock prints, emerged towards the end of the nineteenth century and into the beginning of the twentieth. It was bolstered by Japan's own efforts to expand awareness of its country and wares through participating in world's fairs and expositions, often highlighting gardens and plants.

Like China, Japan exhibited at the Philadelphia Centennial International Exposition of 1876. The Japanese presentation included a garden, which featured a pavilion with a bonsai display. Bonsai were also shown at Japan's exhibition at the Chicago World's Fair in Illinois in 1893, and at the Louisiana Purchase Exhibition in St. Louis, Missouri in 1904. Japan also had a significant presence at the Panama Pacific International Exposition in San Francisco, California in 1915, with an exhibit area more than twice the size of China's. Once again, bonsai were shown, and one tree from the Exposition is known to survive to this day — the Domoto Trident Maple now at the Pacific Bonsai Museum in Federal Way, Washington.

THE UNITED STATES

At the same time that Japan was creating Japanese gardens for world's fairs and expositions, private individuals began to create Japanese-style gardens around the United States. The Japanese Hill and Water Garden at the Morris Arboretum near Philadelphia, the Japanese Garden at The Huntington in San Marino, California, and the Japanese Garden at Maymont in Richmond, Virginia, were created before World War I as private gardens, which were later opened to the public. The Japanese Hill-and-Pond Garden at the Brooklyn Botanic Garden was a public garden from its opening in 1915.

While many people were introduced to Japan through its participation in international fairs and expositions, others made the long journey to the country itself and discovered its distinctive culture in person. Among the individuals who traveled to Japan were the Honorable Larz Anderson and his wife Isabel. Anderson served as Ambassador to Japan under President William Howard Taft, returning to the United States in 1913. While in Japan, the Andersons purchased bonsai at the Yokohama Nursery Co. for their home in Massachusetts, and later bequeathed them to the Arnold Arboretum of Harvard University, where some can be seen today.

Arbor of The Yokohama Nursery Co.

Left Ambassador Larz Anderson bought bonsai from the Yokohama Nursery Co. in Japan in 1913. Later, the company exhibited at the 1915 Pacific Exposition in San Francisco.

Select Japanese Gardens with Bonsai in North America		
Date Created	Bonsai Added	Location
1876		Philadelphia Centennial Exposition, Philadelphia, Pennsylvania
1894		Japanese Tea Garden, Golden Gate Park, San Francisco, California
1911	1968	Japanese Garden, The Huntington, San Marino, California
1911		Maymont Japanese Garden, Richmond, Virginia
1915	1925	Japanese Hill-and-Pond Garden, Brooklyn Botanic Garden, Brooklyn, New York
1918		Hakone Estate and Garden, Saratoga, California
1949	1976	Asian Collections and National Bonsai & Penjing Museum, U.S. National Arboretum, Washington, D.C.
1957	1957	Japanese-style Garden and Bonsai, Hillwood Estate, Museum & Gardens, Washington, D.C.
1958		Shōfūsō Japanese House and Garden, Philadelphia, Pennsylvania
1960		Japanese Garden, Washington Park Arboretum, Seattle, Washington
1960		Nitobe Memorial Garden, University of British Columbia, Vancouver, British Columbia, Canada
1961		Japanese Garden, Bloedel Reserve, Bainbridge Island, Washington
1963		Portland Japanese Garden, Portland, Oregon
1965		Japanese Garden, San Mateo Central Park, San Mateo, California
1972	1977	Sansho'en (Garden of the Three Islands)/Elizabeth Hubert Malott Japanese Garden, Chicago Botanic Garden, Glencoe, Illinois
1973		Japanese Garden, Fort Worth Botanic Garden, Fort Worth, Texas
1974		Japanese Garden, Buffalo, New York
1974		Nishinomiya Garden, Manito Park, Spokane, Washington
1976		Japanese Garden, Normandale, Minnesota
1977		Seiwa'en (Garden of Pure, Clear Harmony and Peace), Missouri Botanical Garden, St Louis, Missouri
1978		Anderson Japanese Gardens, Rockford, Illinois
1979	1987	Ordway Japanese Garden, Como Park Zoo, St. Paul, Minnesota
1979		Shōfū'en (Garden of the Pine Winds), Denver Botanic Gardens, Colorado
1984		Suihō'en (Garden of Water and Fragrance), Donald C. Tillman Water Reclamation Plant, Van Nuys, California
1985		Seisuitei (Pavilion of Pure Water), Minnesota Landscape Arboretum, Chanhassen, Minnesota
1988	1985	Japanese Garden, Montréal Botanical Garden, Montréal, Québec, Canada
1988		Tenshin'en (Garden of the Heart of Heaven), Museum of Fine Arts, Boston, Massachusetts
1996		Rohō'en, Japanese Friendship Garden, Margaret T. Hance Park, Phoenix, Arizona
2001	2001	Roji'en (Garden of Drops of Dew), Geroge D. and Harriet W. Cornell Japanese Gardens, Morikami Museum and Japanese Gardens, Delray Beach, Florida
2001	2001	Garden of the Pine Wind, Garvan Woodland Gardens, Hot Springs National Park, Arkansas
2015	2015	DeVos Japanese Garden, Frederik Meijer Garden & Sculpture Park, Grand Rapids, Michigan

Far left The "Specimens of the famous Japanese minimized trees, above 100 years in pots" featured in the Yokohama Nursery Co. Catalog of 1898 are similar to bonsai brought from Japan by Larz and Isabel Anderson.

Left A Yokohama Nursery Co. Catalog from 1903 features flowering cherry blossoms from Japan on its cover to entice overseas plant buyers.

Below When he visited Japan in 1901, renowned plant explorer David Fairchild photographed a man creating a bonsai at the Yokohama Nursery Co.

David Fairchild was another visitor to the Yokohama Nursery Co. in Japan where he photographed a bonsai being worked on. A plant explorer, he and his wife Marion played key roles in the 1912 gift of more than 3,000 cherry blossom trees from Tokyo to Washington, D.C., the precursor of the Bicentennial Gift of bonsai from Japan. Fairchild introduced many hundreds of plants new to the United States, including soybeans, mangoes and nectarines, and he was a leading proponent of the creation of the U.S. National Arboretum in Washington, D.C.

Interest in Japanese-style gardens and in bonsai languished during World War II when anything related to Japan was considered suspect. Following the war, there was a resurgence of interest because Americans returning from Japan were eager to

introduce their compatriots to the expressions of natural beauty they had experienced there. Bonsai enthusiasts who had hidden or given away their collections during the war brought them forward or reclaimed them. Some formed clubs while others taught bonsai techniques, leading to a broadening of awareness of the art form. Japanese-style gardens also enjoyed renewed popularity after the war, encouraged by Japan which sought to strengthen bonds of peace and friendship. Some of these gardens were developed privately and some were public, often created through "sister city" relationships.

Above left A glass lantern slide by Francis Benjamin Johnston in 1923, 8.26 x 10.16 cm, shows The Huntington's moon bridge five years before the gardens were opened to the public.

Above The Japanese Hill-and-Pond Garden of the Brooklyn Botanic Garden is one of the oldest Japanese-inspired gardens in the U.S. It opened to the public in 1915.

Not every Japanese-style garden or arboretum could include bonsai because they require a major commitment of financial and personnel resources due to their need for daily care and skilled maintenance. The Brooklyn Botanic Garden was one exception: it was given a bonsai collection in 1925. The Arnold Arboretum was another when it received part of the Larz Anderson collection in the 1930s.

Other major public gardens added bonsai to their collections after World War II. The Longwood Gardens bonsai collection began in 1959 with 13 trees purchased from Yuji Yoshimura, who also played a pivotal role in the development of the

national collection at the Arboretum. The Huntington collection began in 1968 with the gift of a personal collection. The National Bonsai & Penjing Museum itself was founded to house the Bicentennial Gift of bonsai from Japan to the United States in 1976. A year later, the Chicago Botanic Garden opened its bonsai collection, followed by other major collections across the country and in Canada.

Today, the National Bonsai & Penjing Museum is proud to show exemplars of the finest bonsai from around the world, brought together to allow visitors to experience nature's most delightful and enchanting qualities as expressed in these living works of art.

SPOTLIGHT ON Dr. John L. Creech

Distinguished horticulturist and plant explorer, Dr. John L. Creech (1920–2009) was Director of the U.S. National Arboretum from 1973 to 1980. A Rhode Island native, Creech's creativity and gardening skills kept him and 1,500 fellow prisoners of war alive in remote Poland during World War II. Returning to civilian life in 1947, Creech joined the U.S. Department of Agriculture's Office of Foreign Plant Exploration. In 1955, he made the first official American plant-hunting trip to Japan after World War II, searching for plants to be used for food crops, pharmaceutical research or ornamental purposes. While there, he met Yuji Yoshimura, leading to Yuji's eventual move to the U.S. where he played an important role in bringing bonsai to Washington, D.C.

An enthusiastic and successful plant hunter, Creech was involved in the introduction to the United States of new varieties of camellias, azaleas, daylilies, chrysanthemums and sedum. Most famously, he found and collected the seeds of a Crapemyrtle (*Lagerstroemia fauriei*) on the remote Japanese island of Yakushima, which became the source of powdery mildew resistance in the modern crapemyrtle hybrids developed at the U.S. National Arboretum.

When Dr. Creech became Director of the U.S. National Arboretum in 1973, he began to imagine what role the arboretum might play in the nation's Bicentennial Celebration in 1976. Inspired by David Fairchild's instrumental role in the gift of flowering cherry trees from Tokyo to Washington in 1912, and relying on his own experience and contacts, Creech thought the gift of a few bonsai from Japan might be possible. The rest is history, as they say, well told in Creech's book, *The Bonsai Saga*, excerpts from which are included as Chapter Seven of this book.

chapter two

Presidential Connections

Below President Richard Nixon is shown at his desk in the White House Oval Office with a bonsai on a table behind him.

Above The magnificent "Mums in the Moonlight" viewing stone was a gift to President Ford from the Nippon Suiseki Association in honor of the U.S. Bicentennial in 1976.

Left A Japanese Red Pine (*Pinus densiflora*), given by Emperor Hirohito, was permitted to be at the White House when he and Empress Nagako joined President and Mrs. Ford there for a reception preceding a state dinner in 1975.

Bonsai from Japan and penjing from China, along with the related art form of viewing stones, have served as diplomatic gifts at the highest possible levels, involving presidents, emperors, kings, ambassadors and foreign dignitaries. Why? Because these beautiful trees and distinctive stones are unique gifts from nature, expressions of a country's culture and sophistication, or rare finds from its territory. After their official presentation in the United States, these trees and stones are "honored" by being included in the National Bonsai & Penjing Museum, where they belong to the public and can be enjoyed by everyone.

In the United States, presidents have taken an interest in penjing and bonsai beginning with President Richard Nixon. He was said to have been given a few penjing trees when he visited China in 1972, though none are known to survive. There is a photograph of Nixon with a small bonsai on a credenza in the Oval Office, giving credence to the legend that says he wanted one there at all times.

President Gerald Ford was given a magnificent chrysanthemum-patterned viewing stone, Tsukiyo Kiku or "Mums in the Moonlight," in honor of the U.S. Bicentennial. This large rock is from Neodani in the Gifu Prefecture of Japan, an area renowned for

Right In 1977, at President Carter's request, bonsai were brought to the White House from the U.S. National Arboretum to make Japanese Prime Minister Takeo Fukuda feel at home.

its chrysanthemum stones, and was donated by the Nippon Suiseki Association. The chrysanthemum is associated in Japan with the emperor and his family, and is an East Asian symbol of long life or immortality.

John Creech mentions in *The Bonsai Saga* how the "Mums in the Moonlight" stone came to the U.S. National Arboretum:

There is an enormous and beautiful chrysanthemum stone in the bonsai collection that originally was sent as a gift to President Gerald R. Ford. How it came to be a part of the National Bonsai Collection is an interesting story. In the fall of 1976, Skip [March] and I undertook a collecting trip to Japan to visit nurseries. While there we met several of the donors of the plants and stones in the collection. At one bonsai nursery in Angyo, we were shown a chrysanthemum stone that was to be sent as a gift to President Ford. Several months later, I asked a White House staff member about the stone and what had been done with it. To my surprise, I learned that the crate was in storage until a decision could be made. We had excellent relations with the horticultural staff at the White House, and I suggested that perhaps the place for it was the National Arboretum Bonsai Collection. Our collection had by now received sufficient status so that the stone was duly delivered and became part of the National Bonsai Museum's collection.

Bonsai and penjing are also used to make foreign visitors feel at home. When President Jimmy Carter and First Lady Rosalynn Carter hosted Japan's Prime Minister Takeo Fukuda in 1977, a bonsai from

Below left Given by King Hassan II, a Japanese White Pine (*Pinus parviflora*), in training since 1832, was presented by the Moroccan ambassador to Mrs. Reagan in 1983.

Below A tiger-stripe stone from Japan's Setagawa River was presented to President Clinton during his visit to Japan in 1998, a Year of the Tiger according to Asian calendars.

Right A gift from Prime Minister Takeo Fukuda, this Trident Maple (*Acer buergerianum*), in training since 1916, is a root-over-rock style, reflecting how trees sometimes grow over rocks in nature.

Japan's Bicentennial Gift was requested for the Oval Office at the White House for the visit. In Carter's welcoming remarks, he noted that the close relationship between the U.S. and Japan after World War II was made possible by "the strength of the Japanese society and also the beauty which has always been characteristic of the arts that exist in the minds and hearts of the Japanese people." This beauty is exemplified by bonsai.

John Creech also mentioned President and Mrs. Carter and their appreciation for bonsai in *The Bonsai Saga*:

The bonsai collection was now on the State Department list of places to bring foreign dignitaries. First Lady Rosalyn Carter visited the Arboretum several times with such visitors, once with Ambassador Togo's wife. As a result, the White House used the collection to good advantage when Japanese Prime Minister Takeo Fukuda later met with President Carter.

The White House staff was informed that Prime Minister Fukuda had a yew tree in the bonsai collection and asked us if it would be possible to have the prime minister's bonsai sitting on the credenza behind the president's desk during their conversation in the Oval Office. We were delighted to comply with the request, and Skip March was elected to take the bonsai to the White House. With plant in hand, he was ushered into the Oval Office with lightning speed to place the plant on the credenza behind the president's desk. But in the location where Skip needed to place the bonsai, there was a model of the historic USS Constitution under a glass dome. The

ship had to be relocated, and this required approval from the Navy. But Skip prevailed and the bonsai was set in place.

The next thing he knew President Carter entered the Oval Office just prior to receiving the prime minister on the South lawn. Skip was introduced and had a brief conversation with the president. President Carter suggested that perhaps the tree could stay at the White House. Skip said very diplomatically, "no, it might die if kept indoors." Then President Carter suggested that perhaps two trees could be left if alternated. Well that idea did not go over very well with Skip and he again politely said, "no, Mr. President," and the president

desisted, much to the relief of the White House Garden staff. Then the president went off to greet the prime minister, and Skip had the opportunity to watch the ceremony from the Blue Room.

Bonsai were also on view at the White House when Prime Minister Keizō Obuchi visited President William Clinton and First Lady Hillary Clinton in 1998. Saburo Kato, Chairman of the Nippon Bonsai Association and a key figure in the donation of the Bicentennial Gift from Japan, was present, accompanying the prime minister, his bonsai student. Obuchi's gift to Clinton in 1998 of an Ezo Spruce collected by Kato in the 1930s and a tiger-stripe stone given by former Prime Minister Hiroshi Mitsuzuka were displayed when Clinton visited Japan. The stone, honoring 1998 as a Year of the Tiger in Asian calendars, is from the Setagawa River area in the Shiga and Kyoto prefectures.

Bonsai from the museum again graced the White House when President George W. Bush and First Lady Laura Bush hosted a dinner honoring Japan's Prime Minister Junichirō Koizumi in 2006. A Eurya (*Eurya emarginata*), in training since 1970, served as a focal point in the Blue Room, while an Ezo Spruce (*Picea glehnii*) and a Japanese White Pine (*Pinus parviflora*) were placed elsewhere.

Other nations also use bonsai as the highest level of diplomatic gifts. His Majesty King Hassan II of Morocco gave President Ronald Reagan and First Lady Nancy Reagan two Japanese bonsai from his personal collection in 1983. The king's Japanese White Pine (*Pinus parviflora*) survives to this day and has been in training since 1832.

The United States also uses trees as national gifts. In April 2012, 3,000 dogwoods were given to Japan in honor of the centennial of the gift of flowering cherry trees from Tokyo to Washington, D.C. The gift was announced by Secretary of State Hillary Rodham Clinton at a dinner for Japanese Prime Minister Yoshihiko Noda held at the National

Below left President Clinton and Prime Minister Obuchi flank Saburo Kato in the Blue Room, admiring a California Juniper (*Juniperus californica*), in training since 1967, and one of the first bonsai to enter the museum's North American collection.

Below An Ezo Spruce (*Picea glehnii*), in training since 1925, was carried on a traditional four-handled tray for its return from the White House to the museum.

Geographic Society. The dogwoods were selected by plant geneticist Richard Olsen, now Director of the U.S. National Arboretum, who took into consideration the soil conditions, temperature ranges and insect pests for the trees to survive in Japan. One thousand dogwood trees were planted in Tokyo and another thousand in the Tohoku region that had been ravaged by the earthquake, tsunami and nuclear disaster in 2011. The remaining thousand were planted at schools and other organizations throughout Japan. The State Department specifically requested that Saburo Kato's Ezo Spruce be exhibited at the dinner, a beautiful reminder of the power of trees and other living art forms to be symbols of peace and international friendship.

Right Eurya (*Eurya emarginata*), an evergreen shrub native to the seacoasts of China, Japan and Korea, made Prime Minister Koizumi feel welcome in the White House Blue Room.

SPOTLIGHT ON Saburo Kato

Saburo Kato (1915–2008) was a respected, charismatic and influential bonsai master. The son of a bonsai master, he grew up with bonsai from his earliest years. He experienced the grim days of World War II in Japan when even gray water was rationed and many bonsai were planted in the ground to survive. After the war, there was a resurgence of interest in bonsai, driven in part by American GI's fascination with the miniature trees.

Kato's leadership of the Nippon Bonsai Association (NBA) included the facilitation of the Bicentennial Gift of bonsai to the U.S. in 1976. In fact, he was instrumental in convincing NBA members to participate by donating trees and coming to the U.S. to teach Americans how to care for the trees properly. He himself came to work on the bonsai in advance of their display at the Dedication Ceremony and returned to the museum on many occasions over the years to give advice on the care of the collection. The museum, in turn, honored Saburo Kato during his lifetime for his invaluable role in making the Bicentennial Gift from Japan a reality by naming one of its gardens the Kato Family Stroll Garden.

In 1989, Saburo Kato founded and served as the first Chairman of the World Bonsai Friendship Federation (WBFF), an organization whose mission it is to bring peace and goodwill to the world through the art of bonsai. Today, the WBFF honors Kato's memory by sponsoring World Bonsai Day on the second Saturday of each May, and at the World Bonsai Convention held every four years. Kato believed that the spirit of bonsai, *bonsai no kokoro* in Japanese, was accessible to people everywhere, that by nurturing bonsai anyone could experience how their love and care creates peace and beauty, a feeling that can be extended to all of nature and the wider world.

Top The Kato Family Stroll Garden honors the long-term support Saburo Kato and his wife provided to the museum and its collections.

Above and right Saburo Kato came to America to prune the bonsai in quarantine, preparing them to be displayed at the Dedication of the Bicentennial Gift on July 9, 1976.

chapter three

Gifts from Japan

An apocryphal story, told in jest, says that when John Creech, the new Director of the U.S. National Arboretum, and Sylvester "Skip" March, the Arboretum's Chief Horticulturist at the time, left for Tokyo in 1975 to receive Japan's Bicentennial Gift, they took only two large, empty suitcases to pick up what they expected would be a few tiny trees. Instead, they were thrilled to find 50 trees waiting for them—one for each state in the U.S.— plus six viewing stones, then astonished to learn there would be three more bonsai added to the group. These additions were gifts from the Imperial family—Princess Chichibu, Prince Takamatsu and Emperor Hirohito himself. The trees and the viewing stones packed in their sturdy crates required an entire Pan Am 707 freighter to ship them from Tokyo to California. Two other planes flew them across the continental U.S., arriving in Baltimore, Maryland on March 31, 1975. The trees were unpacked and placed in a special facility for the

Above Some bonsai from the Bicentennial Gift soak up the sun they need in the museum's courtyard on a summer day, with *koinobori* flags flying, mementos of Children's Day, and crapemyrtles at their peaks.

Right Inspired by entrances to Japanese temples and shrines, the Cryptomeria Walk provides a calming transition from the National Arboretum grounds to the museum's display areas.

year-plus quarantine period Creech had negotiated to make their importation possible.

The Imperial Pine, a Japanese Red Pine (*Pinus densiflora*) in training since 1795, took pride of place as a gift from Emperor Hirohito (1901–1989). It was an unprecedented honor for the emperor to include a tree from the Imperial Collection in the gift to the United States. None had ever left Japan before. Fortunately, Creech and his colleagues realized what an exceptional tree they had received, and they made it possible for the tree to leave quarantine and go to the White House for a dinner on October 3, 1975 honoring Emperor Hirohito and Empress Nagako, hosted by President Gerald and First Lady Betty Ford.

Princess Chichibu (1909–1995), the Emperor's sister-in-law, wife of the Emperor Taishō's second son, gave a tree from her personal collection—a Japanese Hemlock (*Tsuga diversifolia*). The daughter of a Japanese diplomat, Princess Chichibu was born Setsuko Matsudaira in London. Later, her father was

named Ambassador to the United States and she graduated from Sidwell Friends School in Washington, D.C. In addition to her interest in bonsai, Princes Chichibu supported activities involving international good will, health, sports and scholarship, serving for many years as President of the Japan Anti-Tuberculosis Association. The Japanese Hemlock is in the formal upright style and began training as a bonsai in a pot in 1926.

John Creech hosted Princess Chichibu when she visited her tree at the National Arboretum. He described the visit in *The Bonsai Saga*:

One other amusing event occurred in the spring of 1978 during the visit of Princess Chichibu, the Emperor's [sister-in-law], who requested to see her tree and the

Above The Imperial Pine, a Japanese Red Pine (*Pinus densiflora*), in training since 1795, was the first bonsai from the Japanese Imperial Collection to leave the country.

Left Thin bamboo rods provided shade in traditional Japanese style when the National Bonsai & Penjing Museum was new and the Imperial Pine was on public display.

Left Princess Chichibu, Emperor Hirohito's sister-in-law, gave a Japanese Hemlock (*Tsuga diversifolia*), in training since 1926, from her collection as part of Japan's Bicentennial Gift to the U.S.

Top Princess Chichibu visited her gift tree and other bonsai from Japan at the National Bonsai & Penjing Museum in 1978.

Above During her visit to the museum, Princess Chichibu was delighted to find a robin feeding her hungry babies in her nest in the Japanese Imperial Pine.

Above Prince Takamatsu, brother of Emperor Hirohito, added this Trident Maple (*Acer buergerianum*), in training since 1895, to Japan's Bicentennial Gift to America. Its dramatic shape, with a distinctive arching trunk, and changing foliage delight visitors in every season.

Left Before he became emperor, Prince Hirohito was photographed in 1921 with his brothers: left to right, the future emperor, Prince Mikasa, Prince Takamatsu and Prince Chichibu.

pavilion.... Of course the State Department had them on a tight schedule, with an escort determined to keep the visit on track. They had almost completed their stroll through the pavilion, but just as they were about to leave, Princess Chichibu spotted a robin in a nest in the Emperor's red pine tree. Well, I must tell you that the excitement was remarkable.... For a good half an hour, they photographed the robin in her nest and chatted excitedly about this wonderful event, much to the distress of their State Department guide [whose] schedule had just been destroyed.

The third tree with a Japanese imperial connection is a Trident Maple (*Acer buergerianum*), which was trained as a bonsai from a seedling. It was a gift from Prince Takamatsu (1905–1987), the third son of Emperor Taishō. Prince Takamatsu served in Japan's navy through World War II, after which he

played largely ceremonial roles in a variety of activities, ranging from international relations, health and welfare to fine arts and sports. The Prince's tree has a quiet nobility and is treasured for its distinctive curving trunk, its artful roots and its dramatic fall foliage. It is believed to have been in training since 1895.

The other 50 trees assembled by the Nippon Bonsai Association may not have had imperial pedigrees, but each was specially selected from private collections to represent Japan, and some had amazing stories of their own.

The oldest tree in the gift and at the National Bonsai & Penjing Museum today is the Yamaki pine, a Japanese White Pine (*Pinus parviflora* 'Miyajima'), which has been in training since 1625. Its designation as 'Miyajima' shows it is from an island not far from Hiroshima, famous for its torii gate and the Itsukushima Shrine. While the tree was known to be ancient when it arrived in American quarantine in 1975, no one knew its full story until 2001 when grandsons of the bonsai master Masaru Yamaki, who had given it, visited the tree at the U.S. National Arboretum. The young men explained that their family had operated a commercial bonsai nursery in Hiroshima for several generations. On August 6, 1945, the atomic bomb dropped less than two miles from their home, blowing out all of the glass windows. Each family member was cut though miraculously no one suffered any permanent injuries. The Yamaki pine and others in the nursery were protected from the blast by a wall, and its inclusion added a profound and poignant note to the Bicentennial Gift.

Another Japanese White Pine (*Pinus parviflora* 'Miyajima') arrived after the Bicentennial Gift. The distinctive slant of the trunk is balanced by the design of its branches and foliage. It was given to the museum by the late Daizo Iwasaki, a noted bonsai collector in Japan.

A tree treasured by the Japanese is the cryptomeria or Sugi (*Cryptomeria japonica*). It is often called a Japanese cedar though it is not a true cedar. In Japan, some consider it the national tree because it is often planted around temples and shrines, marking the passage from the "daily" world to a "sacred" space. At the National Bonsai & Penjing Museum, cryptomeria line the entrance walk, creating a transitional space into the museum's pavilion area, similar to their use in Japan. Its evergreen quality is perceived as a symbol of

longevity and strength. In addition to its landscape use, Cryptomeria is also used for lumber and for a variety of crafted products. The bonsai Cryptomeria forest planting in the Bicentennial Gift echoes the "grown up" versions lining the entrance walk and was a gift of a former Prime Minister of Japan, Eisaku Satō.

A Trident Maple (*Acer buergerianum*), in training since 1856, has a different shape from Prince Takamatsu's and was included in the Bicentennial

Gift. It was also grown from a seedling but this one conveys majesty in a different way. It has a formal upright-style trunk tapering to an apex with flaring surface roots, creating the illusion of great age and magnificence.

Following his state visit with President Clinton in 1999, Japanese Prime Minister Keizo Obuchi (1937–2000) gave the museum a gift of seven bonsai. One is a 9-inch-high Japanese Zelkova (*Zelkova serrata*) that has been in training since 1984 and

Above The Yamaki Pine, a Japanese White Pine (*Pinus parviflora* 'Miyajima'), in training since 1625, appears to be even older than it is because of the deep fissures in its trunk.

Above left The Yamaki Pine was among the bonsai in the Bicentennial Gift admired by visitors to the National Bonsai Association's headquarters in Tokyo's Ueno Park before being crated for shipment to the U.S.

Below left Descendants of donor Masaru Yamaki, including Shigeru Yamaki shown here, have visited the tree in recent years, keeping alive its remarkable story of surviving the bombing of Hiroshima.

will never grow any larger. Dr. Thomas Elias, then Director of the U.S. National Arboretum, played an important role in the gift, ensuring the museum collections' continued pre-eminence among public bonsai collections in North America.

About 35 of the original trees from Japan's Bicentennial Gift survive today, ably fulfilling their role as international ambassadors. Others have joined them in the intervening decades and others will surely be added in the future, ensuring that the bonsai's expression of the power of beauty, perseverance and peace will abide far into the future.

Above left Cryptomeria trees, considered the national tree of Japan, grow inside the entrance of the National Bonsai & Penjing Museum.

Above A forest planting of Japanese cedars (*Cryptomeria japonica*), in training since 1905, was contributed to the Bicentennial Gift by former Prime Minister Eisaku Satō.

Above A photographer captures the glowing fall foliage of three Japanese bonsai: left to right, a Ginkgo (*Ginkgo biloba*), a Zelkova (*Zelkova serrata*) and a Trident Maple (*Acer buergerianum*).

Above right Although Zelkovas can surpass 50 feet in nature, as bonsai they are only a few feet tall, or, if a *shohin* bonsai like this one, just a few inches high.

Opposite A slant-style Japanese White Pine (*Pinus parviflora* 'Miyajima'), in training since 1879, was a gift of Daizo Iwasaki to the national collection in 2004.

Above An informal upright Trident Maple (*Acer buergerianum*), in training since 1856, seems much older than it really is thanks to its strongly tapered trunk and wide-spreading surface roots.

SPOTLIGHT ON Yuji Yoshimura

While the Bicentennial Gift from Japan provided the impetus toward the establishment of the National Bonsai & Penjing Museum, the trees in that collection were not the first bonsai to arrive at the U.S. National Arboretum. Dr. Creech met and befriended Yuji Yoshimura during his plant explorations in Japan and was instrumental in encouraging Yoshimura's immigration to the United States for a fellowship at the Brooklyn Botanic Garden in 1958, where he cared for their bonsai collection.

Dr. Creech invited Yoshimura to Washington in 1973 to encourage local enthusiasm for bonsai. At a meeting of the Potomac Bonsai Association, Yoshimura stunned the audience with his drastic pruning of a Kingsville Dwarf Boxwood (*Buxus microphylla* 'Compacta'). One attendee expressed her shock at the skeletal form, saying, "Oh dear. He's killing the plant!" Today, more than forty years later, museum visitors can enjoy the results of Yoshimura's masterful technique that established a basic structure for the future training of the boxwood as a bonsai.

Yuji Yoshimura was an animated and committed teacher, working to encourage enthusiasm for bonsai in the U.S. He often used his students' bonsai as examples.

Above Dr. Creech and Yuji Yoshimura considering a Kingsville Dwarf Boxwood (*Buxus microphylla* 'Compacta'), a plant prized for its small leaves and slow growth.

Left On July 9, 1976, during the dedication ceremony, Yuji Yoshimura posed with the Imperial Pine and a Chrysanthemum Stone, both part of Japan's Bicentennial Gift to the U.S.

Below left Crystals form the flower shapes seen in this Chrysanthemum Stone from Neodani in Gifu Prefecture, Japan, which was polished by a river's waters, not by hand.

Below right Created by his father Tohiji Yoshimura in 1930, this Crapemyrtle (*Lagerstroemia indica*) represented a family legacy entrusted to the National Bonsai & Penjing Museum by Yuji Yoshimura in 1990.

Yoshimura's commitment to teaching the principles of classic bonsai techniques and viewing stone principles that he had learned from his father Toshiji Yoshimura was comprehensive. He taught extensively from his home base in Westchester County as well as traveling worldwide. Notably, he preferred to assist his students in creating bonsai rather than establish a collection of his own. He published many articles and co-authored two books, *The Japanese Art of Miniature Trees and Landscapes* in 1957, and *The Japanese Art of Stone Appreciation: Suiseki and Its Uses with Bonsai* in 1984.

Less than two years after Yoshimura's virtuoso performance in Washington, his living work of art would be joined by 53 other trees and six viewing stones from Japan, leading to the creation of the National Bonsai & Penjing Museum.

chapter four

The Chinese Collection

Left The curving top edge of a wall evokes the ripples of a dragon's back and serves as a background for colorful blooms in one of the museum's gardens.

Above The entrance gate to the Chinese Pavilion honors its namesake and primary donor, Dr. Yee-Sun Wu, whose gift of 24 penjing in 1986 made the pavilion possible.

Although the Chinese art form of penjing is older by centuries than the bonsai in Japan it inspired, a large collection of penjing arrived at the U.S. National Arboretum ten years after the dedication of Japan's Bicentennial Gift of bonsai in 1976. Dr. Creech had always intended to include penjing in the Arboretum's collections, but it was his successor, Dr. Henry Marc Cathey, who accepted the gift.

In *The Bonsai Saga*, John Creech wrote:

On his way home [in 1974], John [Hinds] stopped in Hong Kong to meet with Dr. Yee-Sun Wu, a prominent Chinese banker and owner of a famous penjing collection.

Left A Japanese Black Pine (*Pinus thunbergii*), in training since 1936, was shaped by Dr. Yee-Sun Wu in a distinctive flowing style echoed in other Chinese arts.

Below *Lady Under a Gnarled Pine Tree*, ink and color on silk, 16th century, China, 27.8 x 24.2 cm, echoes the sentiment of Dr. Wu's Japanese Black Pine.

The museum's inaugural penjing gift from Dr. Wu and Mr. Lui included artfully stylized trees in pots or *penzai*, similar to Japanese bonsai, and small tree and rock compositions called *penjing*, evoking imaginary landscapes in the Chinese tradition, often celebrating the scholar-hermit. Today at the museum, all the Chinese forms of dwarf trees in containers, with or without rocks, or sometimes using only rocks, are referred to as penjing.

The scholar-hermit enjoyed a privileged position in ancient China. The ideal was that after serving in

Far left A Chinese Elm (*Ulmus parvifolia*) from Dr. Wu has been in training since 1906. If planted in the ground, it could grow to 50 feet or more.

Left A Nepalese Firethorn (*Pyracantha crenulata*), given by Dr. Wu, has been in training since 1966 and changes through the seasons like its full-sized relatives.

Right A gift from Mr. Lui, the Golden-larch (*Pseudolarix amabilis*), in training since 1971, is a deciduous conifer that turns brilliant yellow before dropping its needles each fall.

He had advised Dr. Wu much earlier about our plans for a national collection at the National Arboretum, including the concept of having Japanese, Chinese and American trees. While Wu was impressed with the concept, he hoped that the collection would be located in California. [In a footnote, Creech goes on to say] Dr. Wu undoubtedly was concerned about the colder winters in Washington, D.C. Nevertheless, in 1983, Janet Lanman [a board member of the National Bonsai Foundation] wrote to Dr. Wu to renew our previous request that he donate some of his penjing for display at the U.S. National Arboretum, and Dr. Wu agreed, realizing that the Arboretum would provide adequate winter protection for his trees. In July 1986, ten years after the Japanese Bicentennial Gift, the National Aboretum received a collection of 31 penjing from Hong Kong—24 from Dr. Wu and seven from his colleague Mr. Shu-Ying Lui.

Left Stanley Chinn, a Chinese-American, trained a Trident Maple (*Acer buergerianum*) into a dragon shape. While historically significant, this style is not as popular now as it once was.

Above These images show how one of Chinn's Chinese Elms (*Ulmus parvifolia*) has been trained to create a more windswept appearance over several years.

Below Penjing added to the decoration in the room where President Richard Nixon toasted with Chinese Premier Chou En-Lai during his historic trip to China in 1972.

the bustling world, the scholar-hermit would retreat to an ascetic life, devoted to cultivating art and writing poetry, living close to nature. A penjing from Dr. Wu with a tiny figure beneath a Pauper's-tea tree (*Sageretia thea*), in training since 1951, evokes this dream life, captured in a poem by the eighth century Chinese poet Wang Wei:

> *I sit alone in a bamboo grove,*
> *Strumming on my lute while singing a song;*
> *In the deep forest no one knows I am here,*
> *Only the bright moon comes to shine on me.*

President Nixon saw penjing during his historic visit to China in 1972 and it is believed that he was given some to bring back to the United States, though none survive. It was not until Dr. Wu's collection, augmented by pieces from his friend Mr. Lui, arrived in Washington that the Chinese

art form became accessible to the Arboretum's visitors and they could experience the living arts that had inspired and evolved into the bonsai of Japan.

A Japanese Black Pine (*Pinus thunbergii*) from Dr. Wu's collection is an excellent example of a tree penjing. It has been in training since 1936 and was styled by Dr. Wu himself. Dr. Wu was a master of the Lingnan School of penjing that uses the "clip and grow" method to shape the trees. The curvy lines of this example are typical of Lingnan School work, where the trunk and branches suggest a flowing image. "Clip and grow" stylists do not historically use wire to shape their trees' trunks and limbs.

Chinese penjing are also closely related to other art forms as the image on page 41 of a painting from the Ming Dynasty shows. In it, a lady is seated under a curved pine tree, eerily similar to the Japanese Black Pine in Dr. Wu's living work of art. It is easy to see that the penjing stylist and the painter are aiming

Left Trained by Stanley Chinn in the "Literati Style," a Japanese Black Pine (*Pinus thunbergii*) resembles elements in paintings by Chinese scholars, with its thin trunk and scant foliage.

Right Looking at this landscape penjing of Chinese Elms (*Ulmus parvifolia*), rocks and tiny figures of sages and a fisherman is like viewing a Chinese scroll painting.

to evoke a similar feeling in their works. The only differences are that the penjing is three-dimensional and is made of living materials, whereas the painting is a flat, two-dimensional image depicted with color on silk.

Similar to Japanese bonsai, the illusion of age is prized in penjing. These examples of Chinese Elms (*Ulmus parvifolia*) have gnarled or rutted trunks, typical of ancient, weathered trees. Also like Japanese bonsai, penjing can feature groups of trees, like groves found in nature. The Nepalese Firethorn (*Pyracantha crenulata*) planting was another gift of Dr. Wu. It has been in training since 1966, and it can be relied on to produce small red fruits that last through the winter, followed by fragrant white blossoms in the spring. The Golden-larch (*Pseudolarix amabilis*), a gift from Mr. Lui, is a rare and unusual conifer from China that turns bright yellow in the fall before dropping its needles. This penjing's pot is unique for its depth and red color. It shows how in penjing every element, including the container and the stand, plays a role in conveying the spirit of the whole.

Some of the most eye-catching penjing on display at the National Bonsai & Penjing Museum are the work of Stanley Chinn, a Chinese-American whose ancestors came to the United States to work on the

Above *Pine and Rock*, ink on paper, 18th–19th century, 107.2 x 47.6 cm, China, shares the slim trunk and sparse foliage of "Literati Style" penjing.

Below Past Director of the Penjing Research Center at the Shanghai Botanical Garden, Hu Yun Hua created the penjing at left during an Arboretum symposium in 2004.

railroads. Chinn used many different techniques to achieve his desired result, ranging from historical styles like the Trident Maple (*Acer buergerianum*), trained into a formalistic-style dragon shape, to the Chinese Elm (*Ulmus parvifolia*) that presents a vivid, windswept demeanor. Both the "dragon" and "windswept" penjing are good examples of small trees grown with or over rocks.

Penjing is also known for its "Literati Style" specimens—trees with tall, slender trunks and sparse foliage resembling the types of trees featured in Chinese scholars' paintings and calligraphy. Stanley Chinn's gift included a striking example of the "Literati Style" created with a Japanese Black Pine (*Pinus thunbergii*).

Whole scenes presented on trays of white marble are also considered penjing. The idea is that the viewer is looking at a big landscape, similar to one depicted on a Chinese scroll, only the materials used are taken from nature and artfully arranged to create an imagined vista in three dimensions. A show-stopper of this genre was created by Mr. Hu Yun Hua, former Director of the Penjing Research Center at the Shanghai Botanical Garden in China, when he visited the Arboretum in 2004. The trees are Chinese Elms (*Ulmus parvifolia*) set among stones. The penjing depicts three sages gathered in the midst of a grove and another man fishing

Some landscape penjing have no plants at all, conveying their "story" through the artful selection and arrangement of rocks only. *Spring Rain*, composed of Qi stone from Jiangsu Province in China, was a gift to the U.S. National Arboretum from the Shanghai Botanical Garden, an important partner in the arboretum's plant conservation and exploration efforts.

Above left *Landscape with Tall Trees* by Qian Weichang (1720–1772), painting on folding fan, mid-18th century, 18.4 x 54.0 cm, China, echoes the feel of landscape penjing.

Above A rock-only penjing, *Dancing Dragon*, made of Linglong stone from Anhui Province, China, portrays a mythic shoreline explored by sailors.

The various forms of penjing all evoke an idealized natural world, an imaginary realm where humans take their place within all of nature, including plants, animals and rocks. Because of the upheavals in China in the last century, however, not many antique examples of penjing survive, although images of penjing exist in ancient texts and paintings, confirming that it is an age-old art form. The work of recent and contemporary penjing practitioners is therefore invaluable in bringing the art form to life for audiences around the world.

Right *Peach Blossom Spring* by Shitao (1642–1707), ink and color on paper, Qing Dynasty, 25 x 157.8 cm, China, renders spring weather in two dimensions.

Below A gift from the Shanghai Botanical Garden, this rock-only penjing is made of Qi stone from Jiangsu Province, China. Its smooth surfaces evoke the fresh-washed feel of its title, *Spring Rain*.

Below A Pauper's-tea (*Sageretia thea*) has been in training since 1951. In the wild, the leaves are sometimes used as a substitute for tea in China.

Right Another of Dr. Wu's Chinese Elms (*Ulmus parvifolia*), in training since 1956, seems ready to fly free of its pot, thanks to its elevated roots.

SPOTLIGHT ON Yee-Sun Wu

Dr. Yee-Sun Wu (1904–2005) was a native of Guangdong Province of China who made his way as a teenager to Hong Kong to support his family. He achieved tremendous success as a founder of the Wing Lung Bank. Following family tradition, he became an avid penjing practitioner and amassed a collection of nearly 400 specimens. He espoused the "clip and grow" or Lingnan School of training penjing, meaning that no wire is used to shape the limbs or trunk.

To encourage an interest in penjing, he established a public garden in Hong Kong where visitors could view the tiny trees. He also published two books, *Man Lung Artistic Pot Plants*, that provides a history of penjing in China, and *Man Lung Penjing*, that presents his collection, revealing his distinctive creative style. "Man Lung" means "literate farmer" or "scholar farmer" in southern Chinese, which Dr. Wu may have chosen to describe his ideal.

Before his death, he gave away most of his penjing collection. In addition to those found today at the National Bonsai & Penjing Museum, where the Chinese Pavilion is dedicated to him, examples of his work can be seen in Canada at the Montréal Botanical Garden and at the Dr. Sun Yat-Sen Classical Chinese Garden in Vancouver.

Dr. Wu's influence was truly far-reaching. An asteroid discovered in 1979 in the Main Asteroid Belt between Jupiter and Mars by the Purple Mountain observatory in Nanking, China, was named 3570 Wuyeesun in honor of Dr. Wu in 1997.

chapter five

North American Highlights

The arrival of the Japanese bonsai in 1975 galvanized the interest of the burgeoning group of bonsai enthusiasts and practitioners in the United States and focused their attention on the U.S. National Arboretum. Some were bonsai masters in their own right, others were students of John Naka on the west coast or of Yuji Yoshimura on the east coast or of other bonsai teachers in America. Wherever they were, they were united in their desire to encourage interest in bonsai in North America.

John Naka was among the first to express interest in the bonsai in the Bicentennial Gift. He traveled regularly from California to Washington, D.C. to make sure the trees were cared for properly. He also served as a facilitator for the curator, Robert "Bonsai Bob" Drechsler, with representatives of the Nippon Bonsai Association. They would visit annually from Japan, nod approvingly when they were at the U.S. National Arboretum, then stop in California on their way home to Japan and tell John Naka what they really thought was going on. He would convey their comments to Drechsler, who was grateful for the experts' advice.

The impetus to start a North American collection at the museum came from the Philadelphia Flower Show in 1984 when its theme was "A Trip to the Orient." John Naka came from California for the show, bringing *Goshin*, his prize forest planting of Chinese Juniper (*Juniperus chinensis* 'Femina') to display. Encouraged by Chase Rosade, Naka was convinced to leave *Goshin* at the U.S. National Arboretum's museum, and soon other American bonsai artists offered their work to be considered for inclusion in the national collection.

Goshin was the first of several works Naka gave to the museum. Its name means "Protector or Guardian of the Spirit" and its eleven trees represent his eleven grandchildren. *Goshin* is quite large and it is easy for viewers to lose themselves in the forest glade Naka created, using their mind's eye. In 1990, he also gave a Blue Atlas Cedar (*Cedrus atlantica*), a single tree in a straightforward pot, in training since 1948. He named it *Gimpo* or "Silver Phoenix" because he believed that even a homely tree could become a splendid bonsai, renewed like the mythical phoenix, rising to new life over and over again.

A Thorny Elaeagnus (*Elaeagnus pungens*) was a more recent gift from Naka, arriving at the Museum in 2004. It has been in training since 1960 and has several distinctive features. Its split and gnarly trunk gives the illusion of an ancient tree found in nature. Its front view seems to come forward in space toward the viewer. The back view is equally interesting, revealing more intricacies of its wizened trunk, proof of John Naka's belief that the best bonsai look great from both sides.

Bonsai artists prize Pomegranates (*Punica granatum*) for their twisted trunks, distinctive foliage and twigs. John Naka gave one to his wife Alice, who in turn gave it to the museum in 1990. It has

Right A native plant of the Sonoran and Mojave deserts and southern California, the California Juniper (*Juniperus californica*) bonsai was created by Harry Hirao in 1960.

been in training since 1943 and is an excellent example of a bonsai appearing older than it actually is. By severely tapering the trunk, Naka created the illusion of a superb ancient tree.

Government entities also added to the museum's North American collection. The U.S. Forest Service commemorated its 75th anniversary by giving a Ponderosa Pine (*Pinus ponderosa*) to the museum in 1980. The Ponderosa Pine grows widely in the American west and is the state tree of Montana. The gift to the museum was collected and styled by Dan Robinson, a west coast bonsai artist. In training since 1966, its dynamic shape evokes the adverse weather conditions these trees typically experience in the wild.

Vaughn Banting (1947–2008) was a student of John Naka and an ardent museum supporter. A native of Saskatchewan, Canada, he moved with his family to New Orleans, Louisiana, where they operated a plant nursery. Banting wanted to embark on a career in ornamental horticulture and landscape architecture but his studies were interrupted by service in the Vietnam War, for which he was awarded a Purple Heart. He returned to civilian life in Louisiana and his love of bonsai, and worked with Yuji Yoshimura.

Among his contributions to the museum was a Bald-cypress (*Taxodium distichum*). The Bald-cypress is a deciduous conifer, meaning it loses its feathery needles for the winter. As an immature tree, Bald-cypresses have a Christmas tree-like shape, but as they age they shed their lower branches and their crowns spread, creating an unmistakable flat-top

Above Front (top) and back (lower) views of John Naka's Thorny Elaeagnus (*Elaeagnus pungens*), in training since 1960, show off its twisting, knotty trunk suggestive of great age.

Right John Naka's *Gimpo*, meaning "Silver Phoenix," is a Blue Atlas Cedar (*Cedrus atlantica*) in training since 1948, with an ancient-looking thick, fissured trunk.

Left and below A magnificent Pomegranate (*Punica granatum*), styled by John Naka and in training since 1960, appears to be ancient with or without foliage.

silhouette familiar to anyone who has visited the swamps of America's southeastern states. Banting's bonsai version even features a protruding root known as a "knee," common to Bald-cypresses in the wild.

Other Cypress bonsai in the museum's North American collections includes John Naka's first bonsai, a Montezuma Cypress (*Taxodium mucronatum*). He chose it because of its natural "formal upright" shape, which the tree naturally has before its crown spreads, and because its foliage can change with the seasons depending on its geographical location. The Montezuma Cypress is Mexico's national tree and one in Oaxaca is said to be more than a thousand years old. It can grow to a height of more than 100 feet when it is not being trained as a bonsai.

A forest planting of Bald-cypress and Pond-cypress trees (*Taxodium distichum* var. *distichum* and *Taxodium distichum* var. *inbricarium*) was created by Jim Fritchey and Dick Wild in 1988. They collected trees in southwest Florida, planting them on a natural rock slab weighing one ton. Unless they are side by side, the trees are difficult to tell apart. In nature, Bald-cypresses grow taller and in a wider range than Pond-cypresses, extending beyond the American southeast and Gulf Coast where both thrive west to Texas and north into Illinois and Indiana. Pond-cypresses are named for where they are found, on the edges of lakes and in other shallow waters. Bald-cypresses can live in deeper standing water and are often found in wetlands. This forest planting allows both to show off their changing foliage throughout the year.

Another member of the Cypress family is the Chinese Juniper (*Juniperus chinensis* 'Femina'), which California collectors James and Helen Barrett

Above A Bald-cypress growing in the Atchafalaya Basin of Louisiana, the nation's largest river swamp, shows the flat-top form these trees assume in old age.

Above Vaughn Banting styled this Bald-cypress (*Taxodium distichum* var. *distichum*) in the flat-top form of old Bald-cypress trees found in southeast U.S. wetlands.

Below A forest-style bonsai, in training since 1988, features Bald-cypress and Pond-cypress (*Taxodium distichum* var. *distichum* and *Taxodium distichum* var. *inbricarium*) from southwest Florida, planted together on a rock slab.

used to create a bonsai in 1975 that looks like a lone tree that has been hit by lightning, causing the top to die. This is the same type of tree that John Naka used in *Goshin*, and the Barretts chose to follow his style. Junipers are native to China, Korea and Japan where they can grow to 60 feet.

A Chinese Elm (*Ulmus parvifolia*) is another tree that can grow to 60 feet or more in nature. A forest planting of Chinese Elms begun in 1970 by Marybel Balendonck, a student of John Naka in California, shows how the trees can be grouped together artfully, creating the illusion that strong winds have forced them to lean from right to left.

A Blue Atlas Cedar (*Cedrus atlantica* Glauca Group) also presents an illusion. It appears to be clinging to the side of a cliff, the trunk and branches pulled down by gravity instead of reaching up to the light. In nature, this evergreen conifer is a native of the Atlas Mountains that straddle Morocco and Algeria in North Africa. It can grow to a height of 60 feet and a width of 40 feet.

Created in 1960, the Blue Atlas cascade-style bonsai was a gift to the National Bonsai & Penjing Museum from Frederic and Ernesta Drinker Ballard from Philadelphia. Mr. Ballard was the second president of the National Bonsai Foundation. Mrs. Ballard, a student of Yuji Yoshimura, served as Executive Director of the Pennsylvania Horticultural Society from 1963 to 1981. Many credit her with turning the famous Philadelphia Flower Show into an internationally renowned event.

Above *Autumn Moon at Ishiyama*, circa 1857, by Ando Hiroshige, color ink on paper, 33.97 x 22.23 cm, features trees clinging to a cliff, like cascade-style bonsai.

Right In training since 1960, a Blue Atlas Cedar (*Cedrus atlantica* Glauca Group) given by Frederic and Ernesta Drinker Ballard is a dramatic cascade-style bonsai.

Reaching beyond the nation's west coast, bonsai artistry is well established in Hawaii. A Hawaiian highlight in the museum's collections is a Chinese Banyan (*Ficus microcarpa* 'Kaneshiro') trained by Haruo Kaneshiro (1907–1991) beginning in 1975. Haruo Kaneshiro earned his nickname "Papa" because he is considered by many to be the father of tropical bonsai in Hawaii, and because he was committed to encouraging bonsai for all.

Kaneshiro was born in Okinawa and arrived as a young boy with his family on the Big Island of Hawaii, where they came to work on the sugar plantations. As a young man, Kaneshiro moved to Honolulu where he found work as a waiter, leading eventually to his successful career as a restaurateur there. He discovered bonsai after World War II, when a friend from his days on the Big Island showed Kaneshiro the bonsai trees he had rescued and kept hidden for safety during the war. The owners of anything Japanese found on American soil were regarded as traitors.

Kaneshiro helped his friend sell the secret bonsai and he became intrigued by the tiny trees. Because bonsai masters at the time were a closed group, Kaneshiro taught himself to create and care for bonsai by trial and error, evolving his own style. He did not adhere to strict Japanese styles, believing that each tree played a role in shaping itself.

In later years, Kaneshiro was a staunch advocate of bonsai as a living art form accessible to everyone everywhere. He was generous in sharing what he knew and was also instrumental in establishing the Hawaii Bonsai Association. He was honored in 1990 with a certificate of merit award from the Nippon Bonsai Association. In 1993, the Tropical Conservatory at the National Bonsai & Penjing Museum was dedicated to him.

Opposite In training since 1975, this Chinese Juniper (*Juniperus chinensis* 'Femina') appears as if struck by lightning, killing its top, a look made popular by John Naka's *Goshin*.

Above Marybel Balendonck, a student of John Naka, created this dynamic windswept forest planting of Chinese Elms (*Ulmus parvifolia*) in 1970.

Left Haruo "Papa" Kaneshiro began training this Chinese Banyan (*Ficus microcarpa* 'Kaneshiro') in 1975 to imitate old tropical banyan trees with aerial roots seeming to add "trunks."

Above A Buttonwood (*Conocarpus erectus*) from the Florida swamps, notable for its curvy trunk, was styled by Mary Madison and has been in training since 1975.

Opposite above left Marybel Balendonck watches as John Naka works on a Shimpaku Juniper (*Juniperus chinensis*, var. *sargentii*) in the museum's Yuji Yoshimura Center.

Opposite above right In 2014, the museum commemorated the 100th anniversary of Naka's birth with a special display of his works, including a portrait bust of him by Bonnie Kobert Harrison.

Opposite below John Naka is shown with his forest planting *Goshin*, which means "Protector or Guardian of the Spirit." Composed of Chinese Junipers (*Juniperus chinensis*), it has been in training since 1953.

Returning to the continental U.S., a Buttonwood (*Conocarpus erectus*) is a native American tree found in the swamps of Florida. Its naturally twisted trunks create intriguing shapes prized by bonsai artists. The museum's Buttonwood was styled by Mary Madison, a student of John Naka, and has been in training since 1975. Its common name was inspired by its brownish red fruits that resemble old leather buttons.

Like the continent and nation they represent, the bonsai of the North American Collection are a widely varying group, styled by a spectrum of artists, each expressing their own vision of nature in miniature.

SPOTLIGHT ON John Y. Naka

The contributions John Yoshio Naka (1914–2004) made to encourage the popularity of bonsai in the U.S. were extraordinary. Born in Colorado, he returned to Japan as a youngster with his family where his grandfather, Sadehei, introduced him to bonsai. Naka renewed his fascination with bonsai as an adult after he had returned to the U.S. following World War II and was raising his family in California.

Naka believed that bonsai should be accessible to all and he was one of the first to teach bonsai techniques and principles to English speakers. His two books, *Bonsai Techniques I* (1973) and *Bonsai Techniques II* (1982) are considered masterworks to this day. Naka was one of the founders of the California Bonsai Society and he assisted Saburo Kato in founding the World Bonsai Friendship Federation in 1989, affirming his stated belief that "There are no borders in bonsai. The dove of peace flies to palace as to humble house, to young as to old, to rich and poor. So does the spirit of bonsai."

Naka was a well-regarded and sought-after bonsai teacher, using proverbs to make Japanese aesthetics and principles of Zen accessible to Westerners. One of the proverbs he used was "experience is better than learning." By this he meant that we can understand Zen through personal experience of the life force in both animate and inanimate forms of nature, leading to the development of thought and language around the experience.

In 1984, Naka gave *Goshin* or "Guardian of the Spirit," a forest planting of eleven Chinese Junipers (*Juniperus chinensis* 'Femina')— one for each of his grandchildren—as the first contribution to the North American Pavilion. His magnanimity inspired others to give important specimens and now the pavilion that is dedicated to John Naka is home to a distinguished collection of North American bonsai. Naka's essential role in extending bonsai to the world was recognized by Emperor Hirohito in 1985 when Naka was awarded the 5th Class Order of the Rising Sun, the highest order Japan gives to non-citizens.

chapter six

A Vibrant Museum

Above Water jars for spot watering are located throughout the museum. All bonsai require careful watering, some several times a day in the summer.

Above right Educating bonsai enthusiasts of every skill level is a top priority of the museum.

Below right Non-traditional bonsai containers in the Experimental Design section of the National Bonsai Pot Competition exhibit in 2015 expanded visitors' conceptions of container possibilities.

Opposite The Exhibits Gallery features changing bonsai and viewing stone exhibits in addition to highlighting other Japanese living arts, such as this Sōgetsu Ikebana exhibit.

The U.S. National Arboretum is a living museum where trees, shrubs and herbaceous plants are grown in fields and woodlands for scientific and educational purposes. The Arboretum's National Bonsai & Penjing Museum, however, is set in a complex of buildings that could be mistaken for a "regular" museum except that several of its exhibit areas are open to the sky. Bonsai as a rule are not house plants, tropical trees being exceptions, and the small trees need light and air just like the large trees growing beyond the museum's walls. Also like the big trees, bonsai and penjing need water. Watering is so important and varies so much from tree to tree, depending on the species, age, soil and location within the museum's complex, that on hot summer days much of the museum's staff time is spent watering.

For most of the year, visitors can view the bonsai, penjing and viewing stones on benches and tables that bring them to eye level, as the artists intended. Each living work of art has a front and back, and its container or platform is chosen specially to enhance the visitors' experience of the tree or rock. The trees on view in the museum's pavilions are not on "formal" display. The museum's curator is constantly evaluating the trees to identify when the bonsai and penjing are at their peak, and only then are they put on formal display. For these special presentations, the trees are prepared by covering the soil with moss while their trunks and branches

Right This "Literati Style" azalea bonsai, created by the museum's first curator, Robert Drechsler, is displayed with a waterfall scroll in a spring Satsuki Azalea Exhibit.

Opposite The museum's annual displays include a fall foliage exhibit highlighting bonsai from each of its collections whose leaves change color or fruit at summer's end.

are cleaned and trimmed. An appropriate stand is selected and, if needed, an accent plant is also chosen. They are on view indoors for four days at most, then the process of preparing another tree begins again so the trees can be exchanged.

The museum's formal display areas are the Special Exhibits Wing and the *tokonoma*, both in the Exhibits Gallery. A *tokonoma* is an alcove in a Japanese home where art and other cherished objects are often displayed. These can include pictorial or calligraphic scrolls complementing a flower

arrangement, bonsai or viewing stone. A *tokonoma* is only entered to change the display and it is typical to have a rough-hewn wood pillar on one side of its opening to set its tone.

Like any museum, the National Bonsai & Penjing Museum presents changing themed exhibits to enhance visitors' understanding of bonsai, penjing, viewing stones and related arts like kusamono, ikebana flower arranging and pot competitions. Some exhibits highlight the changing seasons as seen in spring blooms, fall foliage and winter silhouettes.

Left Bonsai are on view year round in the open-air pavilions, then are brought together in special thematic exhibitions several times a year. These are installed in the indoor Special Exhibits Gallery and feature posters like the sampling on this page.

At other times, if a bonsai is simply looking great it is put on formal display in the *tokonoma* accompanied by an appropriate painted scroll from the museum's collection. The Toringo Crab Apple (*Malus toringo*) is popular because it is interesting all year long. It has a dynamic curved trunk with white blossoms in the spring, bright green leaves in the summer, yellow fruit in the fall and a jagged silhouette in the winter. On occasion, exhibits take their themes from the wider world, such as the "Year of the Rabbit" exhibit inspired by the 2011 Lunar New Year.

Viewing stones are often displayed with other Asian art objects to give them a context for an American audience. Chinese scholars' rocks with their distinctive irregular outlines and deep crevices are featured, as are stones from Japan and other parts of the world. A highlight of the viewing stone collection is called *La Bella* ("The Beauty"). This stone was found in Giacopiane's Lake in the Ligurian Alps of northwest Italy, and its gray color is typical of rocks in that area. That the viewing stone so closely resembles the topography of the area where

Right Viewing stones like this one from Lingbi Province in China are included in the museum's exhibits, augmented by Asian plant material, decorative objects and other elements.

Left One Hallowe'en, a Japanese Elm (*Ulmus davidiana* var. *japonica*) from the Bicentennial Gift provided a spooky complement to a flying bats scroll.

Above An Ohara School ikebana arrangement in the museum's *tokonoma* welcomes visitors during cherry blossom time.

it is from enhances its inherent beauty. This gift from Luciana Queirolo Garbini in 2001 underscores the museum's international stature.

Other living works of art from far-flung corners of the world include a Water-jasmine (*Wrightia religiosa*), a tropical tree widely used for bonsai in Southeast Asia. The Museum's Water-jasmine bonsai was a gift from Dr. Tang Quoc Kiet in 2002 and was imported from Vietnam. Its common name reflects its need for water in tropical heat and its blossoms' sweet fragrance.

Many are surprised to find a Bougainvillea (*Bougainvillea glabra*) among the museum's bonsai collections because it is a vine. In fact, most any plant with a woody trunk can be a bonsai. The Bougainvillea has been in training since 1985. Bougainvillea plants are native to South America. They are evergreen in rainy climates and deciduous where there is a dry season.

Chinese Banyan (*Ficus microcarpa*) trees are popular for use as bonsai as is another ficus, the Willow-leaf Fig (*Ficus salicaria*). The latter is an

Above A Mountain Stone of gray rock from the Ligurian Alps in Italy recalls their high peaks and is named *La Bella* ("The Beauty").

adaptable plant, thriving indoors anywhere. Because it grows quickly, it is a good tree for bonsai beginners. The museum's clump-style Willow-leaf Fig bonsai has multiple trunks emanating from a single base. Styled by Helen C. Souder, a student of John Naka, it has been in training since 1974.

Speaking of things "far afield," the National Bonsai & Penjing Museum enjoys broad support among the national and international bonsai community. The Nippon Bonsai Association's essential role in the Bicentennial Gift of 1976 that made the museum possible has evolved into an ongoing relationship, invaluable to maintaining the high standards established by the original gift. Many Americans have supported and encouraged the museum from its earliest days, including bonsai experts and enthusiasts as well as commercial establishments. The National Bonsai Foundation is the umbrella organization that garners support for the museum from around the world. It sponsors exhibits and symposia to broaden awareness of and appreciation for bonsai and related arts, such as the pot competitions that promote expanded possibilities in bonsai containers.

Left Natural malachite from the Lukuni Mine in the Democratic Republic of Congo makes a dramatically verdant Mountain View Stone.

Below A Mountain Stone from Thomes Creek in California has natural white crystals on its top that give it a snow-covered appearance.

Right A Mountain Stream Stone from Japan is displayed under a chrysanthemum moon arrangement in an autumn exhibit.

The museum also serves as a training ground for curators at other top-quality bonsai collections. The bonsai curators at the North Carolina Arboretum in Asheville and at the Chicago Botanic Garden studied bonsai at the National Bonsai & Penjing Museum. The curator at the Pacific Bonsai Museum was assistant curator at the National Bonsai & Penjing Museum for many years. The museum's bonsai education component is ongoing since there is an intern each year who holds the *First Curator's Apprenticeship*. The intern acquires skill and expertise in caring for bonsai by working with the collections under the direction of the curator. Bonsai classes and workshops are also offered to the general public.

The museum includes accent and kusamono plantings to enhance visitors' experience of the bonsai and penjing. Composed of wild grasses and flowers planted in small pots or containers, they are often created to express a season. Other times they indicate a location in the wild. Some bonsai have companion plants that grow in the same container with the tree.

Behind the scenes, bonsai and penjing require work all year round. When the Imperial Pine (*Pinus densiflora*) is trimmed, it requires scaffolding for the museum's staffer to reach its topmost branches. Many of the bonsai at Japan's Imperial Household are large because they are used to enhance enormous spaces.

The Imperial Pine is repotted every five or six years in order to allow room for its feeder roots to grow.

Right High school art students find inspiration in the Museum's Tropical Conservatory during the winter months, especially in the blooming Bougainvillea (*Bougainvillea glabra*), in training since 1985.

Left Water-jasmine (*Wrightia religiosa*) earned its name because of its need for water and because of its blossoms' fragrance.

Above A Chinese Banyan (*Ficus microcarpa*) is a tropical tree, native to South Asia and northern Australia, so as a bonsai it can live indoors in temperate climates.

Below This clump-style Willow-leaf Fig (*Ficus calicaria*) has multiple trunks rising from a single base and has been in training since 1974.

Left A Toringo Crabapple (*Malus toringo*), in training since 1905 and part of the Bicentennial Gift, set an autumnal note for a moon-viewing rabbit.

Right A selection of kusamono created by Young Choe for a 2007 summer exhibition, "The Art of Kusamono." Clockwise from top left: 1) Sand Spikerush (*Eleocharis montevidensis*); 2) Switch Grass (*Panicum virgatum* 'Northwind'), Blue False Indigo (*Baptisia australis*), Bush Clover (*Lespedeza* sp.) and Autumn Sage (*Salvia greggii*); 3) Oak Sedge (*Carex pensylvanica*) and Cardinal Flower (*Lobelia cardinalis*); 4) Geranium (*Pelargonium* 'Vancouver Centennial').

Some people have the misconception that bonsai remain small because they are pot-bound. When a bonsai is repotted, about one-third of the roots and soil are removed before it is returned to the same pot with new soil. Because the tree is tied down and watered, it does not need anchor roots but it does need feeder roots. Repotting allows it to continually generate new feeder roots. As a side note, many trees are naturally shallow-rooted no matter what size they are above ground. They breathe and get moisture from their roots. Generally, 80 per cent of their roots are in the top 18 inches of soil around them.

Adjacent to the museum's pavilions, there is a grow-out space where the trees rest and "take a vacation" from being on view in the public pavilions. Trees, like people, need some time out to just relax.

Volunteers help the museum's staff to care for 300 trees. They provide an invaluable service doing a wide range of work, from assisting with daily maintenance on the bonsai to general garden work within the five different gardens in the museum. The gardens complement the bonsai on formal display and temporary exhibits, and are planned and tended

Left The humble Bellflower (*Campanula rotundifolia*) makes a perfect seasonal companion for the robust Ponderosa Pine as spring slides into summer.

Above A Japanese Edo period porcelain dish from Arita, 7 x 27.4 cm, shows a larger tree with a smaller plant, similar to the effect achieved when accent plants are displayed with bonsai.

Right British bonsai artist Steve Tolley gives an advanced workshop at one of the annual Bonsai Festivals held every May at the museum.

Below In a temporary sales tent during the Bonsai Festival, people can buy bonsai from vendors, plus the pots and tools needed to care for them.

with as much as care as the individual bonsai and penjing. Even the museum's entrance and exit are set in gardens. The Ellen Gordon Allen Entry Garden with its distinctive Japanese Black Pine (*Pinus thunbergii*), a large size of the same variety of tree as some of the museum's bonsai, is at the entrance, and the George Yamaguchi garden of North American native plants is near the exit.

In addition to stunning bonsai and penjing and depending on the season, museum visitors might find a sensational garden in bloom or they might simply enjoy the quiet of snow. Whatever they discover, it will be an expression of the beauty of nature enhanced by human skill and creativity.

Opposite Snow highlights the distinctive foliage pads of the Yamaki Pine (*Pinus parviflora* 'Miyajima') on display in the museum's courtyard.

Left Using a traditional Japanese combination of plants, a pot filled with the seven grasses of autumn marks the change of seasons from summer to fall.

Right Other plants from Asia are often featured in the gardens, such as lotuses, a Buddhist symbol of purity and perfection, grown in large water pots.

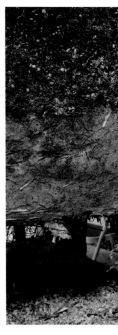

Above left Caring for the Imperial Pine (*Pinus densiflora*) is always challenging because of its large size, designed to enhance spacious areas in Japan's Imperial Palace.

Above right The Imperial Pine is repotted every five or six years to keep it healthy. One-third of its roots are removed before it is returned to the same pot.

Right and far right While many bonsai are small enough to be held in your hands, others require a lot of manpower to move around.

Above left Finding *mycorrhiza* fungi growing with the roots is a sign of healthy soil.

Above center The Imperial Pine's excess roots and soil being scraped away to give the tree's feeder roots more room to grow.

Above right The Imperial Pine replaced in its pot, showing how much soil and roots have been removed.

Right After a bonsai is returned to its pot and its soil replenished, it is watered, an essential element of its daily care.

Above and right The museum's grow-out space is where bonsai are repotted and allowed to rest and "take a vacation" from being on view in the public pavilions.

Above and right Volunteers provide invaluable assistance in caring for the 300 bonsai in the museum's collections as well as performing gardening tasks in its five gardens.

SPOTLIGHT ON Harry Hirao

Above Harry Hirao was happy to be reunited with one of his California Junipers (*Juniperus californica*) in the North American Collection of the Museum.

Above right Harry gives a demonstration during the annual spring Bonsai Festival of how to use wire in training a bonsai.

Opposite Harry stands before stones he collected from the Eel River in California and donated to the museum in honor of his wife Alyce.

Harry Hirao (1917–2015), a longtime friend of John Naka, was a stalwart supporter of the National Bonsai & Penjing Museum and respected bonsai master. He was born in Colorado, educated in Japan and returned to California where he became a pivotal figure in the bonsai community. His contributions to bonsai in America were honored by Prince Takamatsu of Japan and by the Japanese Agricultural Society. His works are distinguished by strong shapes and lines using California Junipers (*Juniperus californica*). In 2004, he gave the museum a California Juniper that had been in training for forty years. Although the trunk appears dead, there is a "lifeline," a thin brown line of living tissue on the underside of the trunk that carries water from the roots to the foliage.

Harry was as interested in viewing stones as he was in bonsai. He gave the museum six stones, three in memory of this wife Chiyoko Alyce Hirao. These stones were collected in the Eel River in northwestern California, an area where Coast Redwoods (*Sequoia sempervirens*), some of the world's tallest trees, are found.

After John Naka's passing, Harry Hirao played the role of "resident expert" at the museum, making regular visits to ensure that the bonsai were properly cared for. His own love for bonsai and viewing stones was so strong it was mentioned in his eulogy when the Buddhist priest cited a sutra and said "Mountains, rivers, grass and trees, all attain enlightenment, [which means that] to an enlightened person a rock is not just a rock, a tree is not just a tree.... An enlightened person can see the innate Buddha nature in all things."

chapter seven

The Bonsai Saga
How the Bicentennial Collection Came to America

by Dr. John Creech

Above Some bonsai are moved around within the museum. Here, the Japanese Hemlock (*Tsuga diversifolia*) given by Princess Chichibu is featured in the lower courtyard.

My first acquaintance with the art of bonsai was in 1947 when I joined the staff of the Division of Plant Exploration and Introduction of the U.S. Department of Agriculture (USDA) at Beltsville, Maryland. In 1898, Dr. David Fairchild established this USDA division for the purpose of sending plant explorers searching the world for new plants for American agriculture.

In a country with only the sunflower, blueberry, cranberry and pecan as native food crops, American agriculture is enhanced by food, feed and fiber plants from around the world. Since its inception, the division of Plant Exploration and Introduction has undertaken well over 200 plant hunting expeditions, and no region of the earth where indigenous crop plants exist has been overlooked.

In conjunction with the collecting of plants by the USDA, there must be facilities to receive introductions, document them, inspect them for pests and finally to grow the great numbers of plant accessions that are received. Seed introductions often went directly to USDA departmental plant breeders or were placed in storage, while collected living plants were required to be grown at Federal Plant Introduction Stations located in different climactic regions of the country.

The Federal Plant Introduction Station at Glenn Dale, Maryland was one such location. The Glenn Dale station served not only as a growing-on facility but also as a main quarantine station for plants normally prohibited from entering the United States. Thousands of valuable plant collections have passed through its greenhouses and nurseries on their way to researchers and nurserymen—the Glenn Dale station functioned as a kind of "Ellis Island" for plants.

One of my first responsibilities was to spend two days each week at the Glenn Dale station to oversee plant distribution and to conduct propagation research. Among the plants being held in quarantine when I arrived at Glenn Dale was a bonsai specimen (either cherry or apple) that had been presented to a high-ranking U.S. admiral by his Japanese counterpart after World War II. It had been in quarantine for about two years under the care of a longtime greenhouse attendant who was an expert at grafting and other methods of propagation. His main goal was to grow plants to perfection before their release, and he took particular pride in this accomplishment. When the day came to release the bonsai, a young naval aide to the admiral came to collect the admiral's plant. It was wheeled out in its diminutive form in fine condition but sporting a new stout branch about four feet high. The proud caretaker commented, "I guess I showed them how to grow a plant properly!" He was actually not far

from the truth because bonsai specialists often allow a vigorous shoot to grow as a way to rehabilitate a weakened specimen. So much for bonsai in quarantine at that time.

Bonsai and Penjing in the U.S. before the Bicentennial

Prior to the enforcement of stringent plant quarantine regulations in 1919, plants entered the United States with few quarantine safeguards and soil was permitted. This included bonsai—or "dwarf trees for table decorations" as one Japanese exporter described them. Japanese bonsai were frequently displayed at national exhibitions but they were often regarded as curiosities.

The famous Boehmer nursery and exporting firm that existed in Yokohama between 1882 in 1908 advertised bonsai in their "original pots" for three to fifty yen, according to shape, age and general attractiveness. There is a sketch in the 1899 catalog of a dwarf maple that was sold to HRH the Princess of Wales. It is likely that many wealthy American visitors returned from Japan with a bonsai or two, but only a few survived or were trained properly.

Perhaps the most successful introduction of bonsai into the United States during the early 1900s was by our ambassador to Japan, Larz Anderson, who was interested in all Japanese art forms. When Anderson returned from Japan in 1913, he brought at least 40 bonsai to Weld, his estate near Boston, Massachusetts, from Yokohama Nursery, the renowned Japanese successor to L. Boehmer and company. His collection was later donated to the Arnold Arboretum where it may be seen in fewer numbers today.

After the plant quarantine regulations went into effect in 1919, the importation of bonsai into the United States became much more difficult. In 1960, when Dr. George Avery, Director of the Brooklyn Botanic Garden, began to acquire new bonsai from Japan to add to the collection which was started in 1925, trees were bare-rooted and fumigated before release to the garden. This treatment almost always killed the plants.

For a time, the U.S. Department of Agriculture agreed to house some of the new bonsai acquired by the Brooklyn Botanic Garden in quarantine at the Glenn Dale station. Later on, bonsai were allowed to go directly into post-entry quarantine at the Brooklyn Botanic Garden, as long as they were free of insects and disease.

One such bonsai that the Brooklyn Botanic Garden acquired from Japan was a famous 900-year-old juniper called "Fudo," which had been purchased in 1969 at considerable expense (perhaps $15,000) by a private donor. The soil had to be removed and the tree was fumigated to meet quarantine requirements. Unfortunately, the tree died as a result of the severe combined treatment. The tree's death sent shockwaves through the Japanese bonsai community and demonstrated that it was fruitless to introduce bare-root conifer bonsai. The skeletal remains of "Fudo" are still preserved

at the Brooklyn Botanic Garden for posterity but this sad event almost caused the Japanese government to oppose the Bicentennial Gift of bonsai.

The art of bonsai continued to be obscure in the United States until after the military occupation of Japan in 1945. Many of the U.S. military personnel, akin to the ancient Japanese samurai, began to acquire a taste for Japanese arts—especially bonsai. Although they were unable to bring plants home because of the quarantine laws, they did have the opportunity to meet many of the Japanese bonsai masters. On returning home they fell in with a few bonsai clubs that formed in various parts of the country, particularly California, Hawaii, New York and Washington, D.C. They purchased seedlings and deformed plants that nursery men would have discarded, and acquired trained plants from Japanese bonsai artists. We owe much to these early bonsai enthusiasts for expanding American interest in this enduring art of Japan.

Regarding the Chinese art of penjing, as stylized dwarf trees are known in that country, even fewer collections existed in the United States. I saw my first penjing in 1974 when I visited the People's Republic of China as a member of the first National Academy of Sciences Plant Studies Delegation to China after World War II. There I was invited to the Lung-hua Nursery near Shanghai where trees, shrubs and flowers were grown for schools, public buildings and street plantings. However, the Lung-hua Nursery is noted chiefly for its collection of several hundred ancient specimens of penjing and as a training school for propagation, trading and culture of dwarf plants.

During this same visit, I had an opportunity to see the famous bonsai/penjing collection of Dr. Yee-sun Wu in Hong Kong, which was arranged by Colonel John Hinds (US Air Force), a prominent American

Above A Japanese Wisteria (*Wisteria floribunda*) was one of the bonsai given to the U.S. in 1976, while other varieties are grown in the museum's gardens.

bonsai enthusiast. The difference in artistic style between the Japanese and Chinese approach was striking—the Chinese style seems strong and severe in character as opposed to the more graceful and reflective style of the Japanese. The reluctance of the Chinese to permit plants regarded as national treasures to be exported, particularly without soil, meant that no penjing entered the United States for decades, except for the collection of several small penjing that were presented to President Nixon at the time of his historic visit to China in 1972.

Until the Bicentennial in 1976, mainly private clubs and amateur growers had advanced the art of bonsai in the United States. Except for the Brooklyn Botanic Garden and the Arnold Arboretum, public institutions were reluctant to develop bonsai collections. This was due to the lack of trained curators to maintain bonsai as well as the cost of plants relative to a fairly limited audience. Today, on the other hand, many arboreta have both a Japanese garden and a flourishing bonsai collection. These institutions have become the support facilities for the many bonsai organizations that have sprung up around the country, and the art has now acquired an international stature.

Plant Hunting in Japan

The 1955 Expedition

In the 1950s, Japan was still recovering from World War II and many bonsai nurseries that had struggled to maintain their collections throughout the war were still impoverished. But they continued to grow and train bonsai with the expectation that better times were coming. Little did they know at

the time that bonsai would become such a popular international art form.

My introduction into the great game of plant hunting was to spend eight months as a USDA plant explorer in Japan in 1955. During that period, I was directed to collect samples of soybeans, rice, fruits, vegetables, and even a rare banana species (*Musa liukiuensis*) native to Okinawa, and to search for plants to be used in pharmaceutical research. The surprising bonus was that I was also authorized to collect ornamental plants. Japan is a treasure house of wild species that are exceptional landscape ornamentals, and Japanese nursery men have selected and improved them over the past ten centuries. Because there had been no serious collecting of ornamentals in Japan since Ernest Wilson of the Arnold Arboretum collected widely in Japan in the years before 1920, I had a gold mine opened to me.

Unlike ordinary governmental travelers, USDA plant explorers were given broad authorization to expend funds. This included hiring conveyances of all kinds (mules, carts, boats, etc.), purchasing necessary equipment, retaining guides importers, and conducting all activities essential to complete the fieldwork. Of course, all such expenditures had to be accounted for, and it must have caused the auditors considerable concern when they received payment vouchers with a thumbprint instead of a signature!

During this first year spent in Japan, I was able to collect over 800 individual lots of seeds, cuttings and small plants that I would regularly ship back home through diplomatic and military air facilities. These collections were packed in sterile sphagnum moss and were flown directly to Washington, D.C., where they were inspected at the plant quarantine inspection house and sent immediately to the Glenn

Dale station. Thus, the timeframe from collecting to greenhouse was only a matter of a few days—in sharp contrast to the months that it been required in earlier days when shipments went by sea.

During this 1955 exploration trip, I also became acquainted with bonsai culture in Japan, particularly azaleas as these were grown by specialists who were solely interested in the large-flowering Satsuki azaleas. The Japanese grew these gorgeous azaleas as potted plants, training them into fantastic shapes. Other growers concentrated on the so-called small-flowered Kurume azaleas for bonsai. Because azaleas are easy to ship bare-rooted, I acquired and shipped back to the United States quite a number of the leading varieties as potential garden plants. Many of these introductions are still in cultivation today.

One of my most constant companions during my 1955 trip to Japan was the distinguished horticulturist Kaname Kato (no relation to Saburo Kato, current Chairman of the Nippon Bonsai Association), who took me to countless Japanese nurseries and botanic gardens. He introduced me to many of the most outstanding examples of Japanese horticulture, particularly the fantastic array of azaleas, camellias, and a rich assortment of ornamental plants held in private collections. During train rides and evenings at small inns, Kaname Kato would describe the virtues of leading azaleas and take me to obscure growers of rare plants whom I otherwise would never have known. We became fast friends, and over the ensuing years we collaborated on the preparation of *A Brocade Pillow*, the English version of *Kinshu Makura*, a treatise on azaleas written in Japanese in 1692.

It was Kaname Kato who took me to the Yoshimura family bonsai nursery, Kofu-En, where I met Yuji Yoshimura for the first time. I later established

a fine relationship with Dr. George Avery of the Brooklyn Botanic Garden, due to our mutual interest in Japanese horticulture. Then, I assisted with his efforts to bring bonsai from Japan, and he would invite me to visit the Brooklyn Botanic Garden on occasion to deliver lectures about my plant collecting experiences in Asia. Through this relationship I was able to add my recommendation that Yuji Yoshimura be employed to teach the art of bonsai at the Brooklyn Botanic Garden.

Little did I realize in those early years of my acquaintance with Kaname Kato and Yuji Yoshimura they would play such an important role in the events that culminated in the Bicentennial bonsai collection.

The 1956 Expedition

I returned to Japan in the fall of 1956 under a new plant collecting program financed jointly by Longwood Gardens in Kennett Square, Pennsylvania and the USDA's Agricultural Research Service. This time the mission was strictly to collect ornamental plants for the American nursery industry. Dr. Russell J. Siebert, Director of Longwood Gardens, was a former USDA plant explorer and believed that ornamental plants deserved equal treatment with other economic crops. When this joint program was finally terminated in 1972, 13 ornamental expeditions to various parts of the world had been undertaken.

My 1956 expedition emphasized southern Japan because of the extensive array of broad-leaved

Left When Kyuzo Murata, Curator of the Imperial Bonsai Collection, visited the bonsai in quarantine, he checked all of them, not just the Imperial Pine.

evergreen species in many interesting localities that had not been visited for decades. One of our goals was to explore the remote Island of Yakushima, some 90 miles south of Kyushu. Yakushima is home to some 1,200 species found in higher elevations, including wild camellias, azaleas, hollies and other plants of considerable interest to the United States. Ernest Wilson visited this island in 1914, and considered it to be a plants man's paradise.

On its highest peak, Miyanouradake (6,348 ft. elevation), colonies of the important *Rhododendron yakusimanum* flourish. It was on Yakushima, along a boulder-strewn stream, that I collected seeds of the rare *Lagerstroemia fauriei*, a crapemyrtle that was destined to become the source of powdery mildew resistance in all of the northern hybrids developed by the late Dr. Donald R. Egolf of the U.S. National Arboretum. The cultivar "Natchez," a superb white-flowered tree developed by Egolf, is now the most widely cultivated crapemyrtle because of its disease resistance and handsome

cinnamon-color bark—both characteristics drawn from *Lagerstroemia fauriei*.

The season also coincided with the great autumn chrysanthemum exhibition where I was introduced to chrysanthemum bonsai. These popular exhibitions also featured large tubs of individual plants trained in precise pyramidal form with as many as 1,000 large ball-type flowers, as well as cascade displays reaching to seven feet and striking displays of historic figures dressed in live chrysanthemums. Growers from each exhibition assembled cuttings of the most highly recommended chrysanthemum varieties, and I arranged to pick them up in late December to carry them home personally. Many plant collectors prefer this approach as a guarantee that their precious cargo will arrive home safely. One spider-type chrysanthemum that I brought back, "Tokyo white," was said to have grossed over $1 million in the nursery industry during its several years of popularity.

The 1961 Expedition

I returned to Japan in 1961 to continue exploration, this time in central and northern Japan. Seeking improved hardiness, the strip focused on the northern range of distribution for both wild and garden forms of our leading nursery species, including azaleas, camellias, hollies other broad-leaved plants and conifers. One important plant we discovered was the northern form of *Juniperus conferta*, the shore juniper that I named "Emerald Sea."

A Bicentennial Gift

The Potomac Bonsai Association 1973 Spring Show

It was not until I became Director of the U.S. National Arboretum in 1973 that I gave serious thought to the possibilities that could result from my earlier encounters with the Japanese bonsai community. What triggered my interest was a meeting with the members of the Potomac Bonsai Association during their 1973 spring show held at the U.S. National Arboretum.

In the spring of 1973, the Department of Agriculture requested its various units to submit proposals for a Bicentennial program. I felt that the National Arboretum in our nation's capital would be a splendid site for an educational display of the wealth of America's agricultural crops, including ornamentals, in a series of demonstration exhibits. This was to be an elaborate project with several permanent features, including a National Bonsai Garden, because the art was gaining popularity across the country, and a National Herb Garden displaying medicinal, culinary, dye, fragrance and related plants. It was my hope that national plant societies would hold their meetings at the National Arboretum during the Bicentennial year.

This was an overly ambitious project but the various local plant clubs and societies that used the Arboretum were quite willing to support the idea. Because Congress had not funded a significant Department of Agriculture celebration in the Bicentennial, the Arboretum proposal went nowhere, and I was left to my own devices as to how the National Arboretum would participate in the festivities for our nation's 200th birthday.

At the 1973 spring show of the Potomac Bonsai Association (PBA) at the National Arboretum, I discussed with John Hinds the possibility of obtaining a small collection of bonsai from friends in Japan for exhibition at the Arboretum. But how would we get the plants here safely? John suggested that the Air Force might be persuaded to fly the plants from Japan since they had regular cargo flights that often returned empty or with partial loads. Other members of the PBA quickly gave their wholehearted support to my idea of a possible bonsai collection at the Arboretum. But still, there were many problems to be solved.

Getting USDA Approval

As a first step, I approached Ivan Rainwater of the USDA plant quarantine agency to see if it would be possible to bring in a collection of bonsai and soil from Japan. There were many genera that were prohibited from entry (including cherry and apple) and, of course, the first answer was "no soil." Our quarantine officials had not forgotten the disastrous importation of cherry trees in 1910 that were so badly infested with unwelcome pests that 2,000 trees had to be burned within sight of the Washington Monument.

However, Rainwater had been the quarantine officer in Hawaii when I went there in 1962 to visit the botanic gardens and we became good friends. Fortunately, he had been transferred to the plant quarantine facility in Hyattsville, Maryland. He gave me approval to go ahead, with my assurance that the plants were going to detention in the quarantine houses at Glenn Dale for a year and be subject to rigorous periodic inspection for possible insects in the soil or diseases. This USDA approval to import

bonsai with their soil was an exceptional departure from quarantine regulations. Nevertheless, it seemed to be a small risk because we agreed at the time that the bonsai would not leave the Arboretum once they were released from quarantine.

Nippon Bonsai Association's Reply

With this concession, I wrote to Kaname Kato on May 11, 1973, and asked whether, in light of the celebration of our 200th anniversary of the United States in 1976, he thought it would be possible for the government of Japan or some representative

organization to make a presentation of a bonsai collection as a symbol of our mutual admiration for living plants. I added that I needed some assurance before I broached the subject with Mr. Talcott Edminster, our Agricultural Research Service Administrator, and loyal supporter of the Arboretum.

Back came a letter from Kaname Kato stating that the President of the Nippon Bonsai Association, Mr. Nobusuke Kishi (a former Prime Minister), was personally very agreeable and willing to explore the idea. I approached Mr. Edminster informally and showed him Kato's letter. He gave his approval to go ahead and assured me that, if the plan were successful we could build a viewing pavilion at the U.S. National Arboretum.

In early June 1973, Kaname Kato met with the directors of the Nippon Bonsai Association (NBA) at the Satsuki (azalea) bonsai show. The NBA directors agreed to accept my request, stating that we "will be glad to send bonsai to your Arboretum to celebrate the 200th anniversary of the United States." From then on, my main contact with NBA was Nobukichi Koide, President and Director of the NBA.

At this point, I could only maintain my composure by reminding myself that my predecessor, David Fairchild, had found himself pretty much in the same boat working both ends from the middle when he acquired the flowering cherries that grace the Tidal Basin in Washington, D.C.

Left Although no longer living, this azalea (*Rhododendron* 'Shi-o') was one of five Satsuki azalea bonsai from the 1976 Bicentennial Gift, shown blooming profusely in quarantine.

Right A Chinese-quince (*Pseudocydonia sinensis*), in training since 1875, bears large fruits in spite of its small size.

Support from the ABS and BCI

Other than the members of the PBA, particularly John Hinds and Jim Newton, the American bonsai world was unaware of our plans to bring a bonsai collection to the National Arboretum. Fortuitously, both the American Bonsai Society and Bonsai Clubs International were to meet for a joint Bonsai Congress in July 1973 in Atlanta, Georgia. John Hinds spoke to the presidents of the two societies and the congress chairman, and they blocked out 10 minutes at the main banquet so I could put forth the concept of a National Bonsai Center at the U.S. National Arboretum. Among those attending the congress was Yuji Yoshimura, who had expressed earlier his dream that the richest nation in the world should have a national bonsai collection.

Following my presentation to the congress, some members of the audience were skeptical about the realistic possibilities of a national bonsai collection. After all, since neither the Arboretum staff nor I had any experience with bonsai, how would we manage such a bonsai collection? Nevertheless, both Dorothy Young, President of the American Bonsai Society, and Beverly Oliver, President of Bonsai Clubs International, signed a resolution dated July 21, 1973, extending wholehearted support for the establishment of a national bonsai collection at the National Arboretum.

This action was an important step since I was then able to advise my Japanese colleague, Kaname Kato, of the support of both the leading bonsai societies in the United States as well as of Yuji Yoshimura. I also

informed our Agricultural Attaché at the American Embassy in Tokyo, David Hume, of my intentions and the status of our plans. I had developed good relationships with our embassy staff in Japan during my several visits, and explained the benefits to U.S./Japan relations if we were to succeed in this endeavor. Hume was enthusiastic about the project and expressed his support.

Logistical Obstacles

With the USDA and the American bonsai societies on board, it was now time to turn attention to the logistics of the plan. Mr. Edminster, the ARS Administrator, told me that there would be only limited funds to construct a bonsai pavilion to house the collection. There was a dollar limit on

construction without congressional approval, and he could not go to Congress to obtain a special appropriation because of higher departmental priorities. Nevertheless, I was quite happy to work within the funding limitations he could make available.

I was now able to advise the State Department that plans for a major bonsai gift from Japan in commemoration of the Bicentennial were progressing rapidly. John Hinds, Jim Newton and I met with the Cultural Affairs staff of the State Department to explain that, while we had assurances that the bonsai gift from Japan was a reality there still was the matter of transporting the plants from Japan safely. We expressed our hope that the Department of Defense might be persuaded to provide space on their cargo flights from Japan.

Hinds, now the Director of Community Relations for the Air Force, was in a position to exert his influence. In October 1973, he drafted a memorandum to the Assistant Secretary of Defense and recommended that the project be given serious consideration on the basis that it would help our relations with Japan considerably. In response to Hinds' memorandum, I received a letter from the Department of Defense asking for a specific request. With approval from my own agency, I wrote to the Deputy Assistant Secretary of Defense, outlining our needs, justification and everything else I could think of to convince them of the significance of the gift. The response was not at all encouraging. Questions were raised about using defense resources for non-defense traffic, about obtaining certification that commercial transportation was unavailable and other similar roadblocks. But the letter did state that, when the specific request was made, possible exceptions to governing restraints would be considered.

A Visit with Henry Hohman

A great boost for the project came in September 1973 when I learned that Yuji Yoshimura was to put on a demonstration of bonsai training at the Brookside Gardens, Wheaton, Maryland. This provided an opportunity to solidify Yuji's support for having a national bonsai collection at the National Arboretum, a place he had never visited. So I persuaded him to come to the National Arboretum to discuss the bonsai matter and perhaps give a demonstration. Yuji agreed and indicated he wanted to use a Japanese boxwood for this program. I knew just the place to find the right specimen.

Henry Hohman was the owner of Kingsville nursery, Kingsville, Maryland, and one of those early plantsmen who really knew plants. I first met Henry in 1947 because his nursery was one that received and tested plant introductions that the USDA distributed regularly. He could be a difficult character and was reluctant to deal with those who were not serious plants people. Among the many introductions Henry evaluated, he was particularly interested in broad-leaved evergreens and had an extensive collection of the Japanese boxwood (*Buxus sempervirens*).

It was out of Henry's boxwood collection that the popular "Kingsville Dwarf" cultivar was selected. Some of these were astonishingly aged specimens, probably up to 50 years old. I arranged for a visit to Kingsville Nursery with Yuji to see what we could find. Bonsai artists Marion Gyllenswan, John Hinds, Jim Newton and Clifford Pottberg came along.

At this time, Henry was desperately ill with cancer and was generally not receiving visitors to the nursery. But he graciously made an exception

Left Yuji Yoshimura worked on a Kingsville Boxwood (*Buxus microphylla* 'Compacta'), a plant prized for its small leaves and slow growth.

for us. After a general tour of the nursery, Yuji began to inspect various box plants but none satisfied him. Finally, Henry said he had some special plants around his residence and asked if Yuji would like to see them. There Yuji found a beautiful, compact plant which was just what he wanted, and Henry promptly had it dug and burlapped. This plant was a propagation of one of the original Kingsville dwarf box plants that Henry had obtained in 1923.

John Hinds had researched the origin of the Kingsville dwarf boxwood. It was discovered in 1913 as a sport by Mr. Sam Appleby, who lived a few miles north of Kingsville. Mr. Appleby nurtured the sport and by 1923 had ten plants. He died in 1923, which was the same year that Henry established his nursery. Henry knew about the ten little "Kings" and acquired them that same year. He was aware that these extremely dwarf plants would never be cost-effective nursery stock—they were too slow-growing and the stems were too brittle. Despite these drawbacks, Henry continue to propagate the material and sometimes sold specimens to wealthy estate owners who used them as dwarf hedge material in their formal gardens.

After a sad farewell, since Henry was in considerable pain, we returned to Washington. That evening

at Brookside Gardens, Yuji entertained a small audience with his masterful techniques. He could be an amusing character, and began his pruning on this well-branched plant by asking the audience: "Should I clip this branch? Or, how about this one?" By the time he had reduced the boxwood to practically a skeleton, one elderly lady in the audience explained, "Oh dear. He's killing the plant!" But, of course he really was just establishing the basic structure for the future training of the boxwood as a bonsai.

From then on, it was Bob Drechsler who cared for this first one of the many bonsai to go into the American collection at the National Arboretum. After this demonstration, Yuji seemed more convinced than ever that we could succeed in obtaining a Bicentennial gift of bonsai from the Japanese.

Support from Colonel Hinds

As 1973 came to a close, I continued exchanging letters with my friend, Kaname Kato, and with Mr. Koide of the Nippon Bonsai Association to determine what was happening on the Japanese side. Apparently they were appealing to the Japanese government and the semi-private Japan Foundation for financial support. While the NBA was totally behind the idea of a Bicentennial gift of bonsai to the United States, I was advised that it was too late for the project to be included in the government's 1973 budget, but there was hope that it could be included in the 1974 budget. I had, of course, already convinced my own administration that we were going to receive a bonsai collection and that we should go forward with our plans for a pavilion to house the plants.

It was also unsettling that, in early 1974, we still had no answer on the use of an Air Force aircraft. John Hinds, however, remained optimistic the transport would be available, knowing that planes often came back from Japan with little or no cargo. I was not so certain, but there was no turning back. John decided to take the transportation matter to Air Force Lieutenant General Maurice Casey, who was the most senior logistics officer in the Department of Defense. General Casey was on the staff of the Joint Chiefs of Staff where he was the "final word" on such logistics matters. Col. Hinds had known the general for a number of years, and they had a good working relationship.

Casey told Hinds that he appreciated the public relations benefit to the Air Force if that service flew the trees from Japan. He was concerned, however, that if the Air Force shipped the trees, the commercial airlines might lodge a complaint with Congress. At that time, the airlines were still up against high fuel costs caused by the 1973 energy crunch and wanted to maximize the use of their airplanes to increase revenue. Still, everyone hoped that the American Embassy in Japan would use its powers of persuasion in Washington to further our cause.

In February 1974, our stalwart supporter, Hinds, arranged to go to Japan for a major bonsai exhibit. He carried credentials from the American bonsai societies to speak on behalf of the bonsai project. I wrote our Agricultural Attaché in Tokyo alerting him to John's visit. Dorothy Young also went to Japan for the bonsai exhibition and spoke eloquently at the meeting about our plans. Yuji had written to his brother, Kanekazu Yoshimura, explaining that Hinds

was coming to Tokyo to help emphasize the sincerity of the United States' position in moving forward with the bonsai project. The younger Yoshimura took Hinds in tow for the entire week of the Ueno Park bonsai exhibition, introducing him to the Nippon Bonsai Association officials and senior bonsai owners.

As it happened, John was acquainted with the senior editor of the U.S. military newspaper, *Stars and Stripes*, which had its head office in Tokyo, and the editor agreed to assign a reporter/photographer team to explore a story about his mission. John told Kanekazu Yoshimura that there was the possibility of a feature story about the mission, including photographs of bonsai personalities at the exhibition. Within hours Yoshimura had permission from the Nippon Bonsai Association to take photographs at the exhibition, and two or three days later a *Stars and Stripes* photographer/reporter team was posing

Hinds and Yoshimura next to a 250-year-old Juniper. NBA's granting of permission to do this sort of thing represented a rare and generous gesture, for traditionally they strictly enforced a "no photography" policy during their exhibitions. Before he left Japan, the *Stars and Stripes* printed a feature story headlined "Colonel Turns Bonsai Diplomat."

On his way home, John stopped in Hong Kong to meet with Dr. Yee-sun Wu, a prominent Chinese banker and owner of a famous penjing collection. He had advised Dr. Wu much earlier about our plans for a national collection at the National Arboretum, including the concept of having Japanese, Chinese and American trees. While Wu was impressed with the concept, he hoped that the collection would be located in California....

On their return, both John and Dorothy reported that the Nippon Bonsai Association was fully committed to assembling a first-class collection of

Right The bonsai in the Bicentennial Gift on view at the Nippon Bonsai Association's headquarters in Ueno Park in Tokyo in March 1975.

bonsai but the negotiations for funding were moving very slowly. Meanwhile, at the Arboretum I began to work informally with architects on plans for a pavilion but could go no further until we had the collection secured. I wrote to Mr. Koide of the Nippon Bonsai Association, assuring him of my complete confidence in his efforts and that he could count on our fulfilling our part of the agreement.

Meeting the NBA Directors in Tokyo

In August 1974, I was part of the first delegation of biological scientists to go to the People's Republic of China and had approval from Mr. Edminster to conclude the trip with a stopover in Tokyo to discuss the bonsai project. Things seem to be breaking just right because I never would have obtained approval for a trip to Japan solely for this purpose. I planned to have the artist's sketches of

the pavilion to show the Nippon Bonsai Association Directors, hoping that this would impress on them the seriousness of our intentions. In addition, Hinds had written to Dr. Wu about my trip and, as a result, I was invited to visit Wu's penjing collection and discuss our plans for a national bonsai and penjing collection.

While in China, we visited many experimental stations, universities and other research facilities. At one point, I was able to break away to go to the Lung-hua Nursery near Shanghai where I had a chance to see and photograph their fabulous collection of penjing. When we returned to Hong Kong from China, I visited Dr. Wu's impressive rooftop penjing garden, which was displayed under tight security. While the rest of the delegates returned home, I flew to Japan for my first face-to-face meeting with the Directors of the NBA since we had initiated the idea.

Left Nippon Bonsai Association members preparing the trees for their dedication in 1976. Left to right: Eijiro Hiruma, Nobukichi Koide, Tsunekazu Nakajima and Saburo Kato.

Earlier, the USDA had commissioned an artist's sketch of our proposed bonsai pavilion and the sketch was completed while I was in China so I had no opportunity to see it. It was sent to our Agricultural Attaché in Tokyo and I picked it up just before the meeting. On September 27, 1974, I arrived at the offices of the Nippon Bonsai Association with my friend Kaname Kato and faced a group of "gentlemen of Japan," solemn faced, mostly elderly and in a very formal setting around a table. None of them spoke English to any extent and we conversed through an interpreter, Miss Junko Arima. This young woman handled most of our exchanges over the next several months and exerted quiet but strong influence on the negotiations.

I explained to them the goals of our plan. It was to communicate by the gift of bonsai how the Japanese people appreciate nature through the enduring art of bonsai and to encourage a similar appreciation of this ancient art by Americans. I described how we planned to construct a pavilion at the Arboretum designed by Sasaki Associates, a famous Japanese-American architectural firm, to house the collection. I laid out the artist's concept of the structure, which I had just seen for the first time.

After my Japanese friends saw the plan, they raised some serious concerns. They asked how the bonsai would flourish in the enclosed environment shown in the sketch, noting the apparent lack of air movement, sunlight and similar environmental needs. I quickly assured them that this was only an artist's sketch and that we would deal with those problems when the architectural firm went to work.

Their main concern, of course, was to be sure that the precious bonsai would receive proper care at the Arboretum. To this question, I said we would appoint a trained curator for the collection and that

Right Robert "Bonsai Bob"Drechsler, the first bonsai curator, caring for the trees of the Bicentennial Gift in quarantine in Glenn Dale, Maryland.

Below right Inspecting the trees in quarantine in 1975, Dr. Creech accompanied Kyuzo Murata of the Imperial Collection and Hideo Chugun and Nobukichi Koide of Japan's Nippon Bonsai Association.

bonsai specialists like Yuji Yoshimura and John Naka had expressed their willingness to serve as advisers and to assist in the training and maintenance of the collection.

With the Nippon Bonsai Association Directors' questions seemingly answered to their satisfaction, there were smiles all around, and Mr. Koide spoke for the Directors saying that they would vigorously implore the various Japanese government agencies for funding. Then they asked when was the best time to send the collection and how would it be done. We all agreed that the early spring of 1975 would be the best time of year because the trees would be dormant and they would have to remain in quarantine for a full year prior to the 1976 Bicentennial. As for transportation, I explained that we were in contact with our Air Force officials and it was most certain the proper arrangements would be made for the safe journey to the United States. At this point it would have been improper to give a more definite answer and they seemed satisfied. I also assured them that the soil in the bonsai containers would not in any way be disturbed. This was an important point because they were aware that in previous shipments of plants the soil had been removed and they knew this was fatal to the bonsai.

So I departed with their pledge ringing in my ears that they would work earnestly to acquire the best bonsai. I, in turn, assured them that I would work equally hard to create a suitable home for these "children of Japan" at the National Arboretum. Before he departed, Mr. Koide mentioned that there would likely be a problem in choosing candidate plants. With so many famous bonsai growers, it was important that a great deal of diplomacy be used in the final selection. As it turned out, several former prime ministers as well as other high officials of the Japanese government would be listed as the donors of bonsai.

I later found out that the death of "Fudo," the large Juniper whose soil had been removed when it was imported by the Brooklyn Botanic Garden from

Japan, had apparently caused the Japanese Ministry of Foreign Affairs to initially oppose my request for a gift of living trees because Ministry officials thought the trees would die. This negative position was reversed after the Ministry realized that the bonsai to be given as a Bicentennial gift could be imported into the United States with their soil intact.

Saburo Kato, who today is the Chairman of the Nippon Bonsai Association and the most respected bonsai master in Japan, was working behind the scenes in those fateful early days. I later learned that Mr. Kato was instrumental in arguing our case before the Ministry of Foreign Affairs. He was able to convince Ministry officials that the bonsai for the Bicentennial gift would flourish in the United States, not only because they would be imported with their soil, but also because the NBA would show us how to care for the bonsai.

Choosing a Bonsai Curator

I returned home and reported the considerable degree of success in my mission to Mr. Edminster and to the bonsai societies. Up to this point we had not given serious consideration to selecting an Arboretum staff member to become the curator of the collection. Our senior horticulturist at the Arboretum, Sylvester "Skip" March, informed me that one of our senior technicians, Robert Drechsler would like to be considered for the position.

Bob was, without question, the right person for the job. He had worked for many years under the strict leadership of our renowned plant breeder Donald Egolf, and "discipline" was Don's middle name. Bob was not only a well-trained horticulturist but had even been caring for the small collection of penjing that had been presented to President Richard

Nixon during his visit to China. Thus, Bob was temporarily assigned the role of bonsai curator so that he could be prepared for the maintenance of the collection when it arrived at Glenn Dale. The year 1974 ended with everyone still awaiting the word that the Japanese collection was a fact.

The Gift Takes Shape

NBA Selects Bonsai and Suiseki

On January 30, 1975 Koide-san wrote that the Japanese government had funded the project. "Now," he said, "we must move quickly to begin collecting bonsai from all over Japan so that they may be sent by the end of March." A team from the Nippon Bonsai Association was then visiting bonsai growers throughout Japan to select the trees to be sent.

Fifty trees would be selected by the NBA—one for each of the American states. The tree selections were intended to express the broad range of plants that were cultivated as bonsai, as well as those of a venerable age and interesting habit. In addition, the gift would include a bonsai from the Imperial Household Agency collection and one each from Prince Takamatsu and Princess Chichibu. In all there would be 53 bonsai.

In addition, six selected viewing stones (*suiseki*) would be sent as an additional gift. The art of suiseki is an important element of bonsai displays. Suiseki are aesthetically pleasing stones that have been shaped over centuries by water torrents or other natural causes. They may be small enough to hold in one hand or so large that they require more than one person to lift them. They may have

irregular white quartz veins running through black basalt to suggest a gushing mountain stream. They may resemble volcanic peaks or even a remote island rising from the sandy beach.

One of the most sought after suiseki is the "chrysanthemum stone" called *kikkaseki*. Mineral crystals formed on the face of the stone resemble an open chrysanthemum flower. This is of great significance to the Japanese as the chrysanthemum is the crest of the Imperial Family. Mr. Kiyoshi Yanagisawa donated the chrysanthemum stone

Above and right A 200-year-old Japanese Black Pine (*Pinus thunbergii*), chosen to reflect the age of the United States on its Bicentennial, was given the place of honor in the main *tokonoma* in the last Tokyo exhibit, accompanied by a Mountain Stream Stone, also part of the Gift.

presented to us. It was one of two such stones that he regarded as "husband and wife." He said that while he was sad to be separating them he was proud that the "wife" would be happy in America.

A Disappointing Response

The ball was now in our court. Up to this point, I had pretty much been taking the lead, keeping Talcott Edminister and other officials well-informed. Our plant quarantine officer, Ivan Rainwater, who approved the list of species to be imported, and our Agricultural Attaché in Tokyo,

Larry Thomasson, who would be our contact with the NBA, were also advised of the progress. I had brought the national Arboretum's chief horticulturist, Skip March, into the picture earlier and now it was clear that he would play a significant role in coming events.

Thomasson cabled from our Tokyo Embassy that he had met with representatives of the Nippon Bonsai Association and that they were making final arrangements for outstanding bonsai candidates from all over Japan. He also said that a formal presentation ceremony in Tokyo was being planned for March 20, 1975, and that it was important for

me or others from the Arboretum to attend the ceremony and fly back to the U.S. with the plants. Our most critical question at this juncture was whether the Air Force intended to transport the bonsai collection.

On February 27, 1975, our Defense Attaché in Tokyo cabled the Secretary of Defense requesting the transportation be authorized to transport the bonsai from Yokota Air Base to Andrews Air Force Base outside Washington.[5] He pointed out that the extent of interest by the Japanese government in the donation to our Bicentennial, the estimated value of the collection ($5 million), and our own Embassy's strong endorsement of the request. But the Defense Department finally turned down the request, despite vigorous pleas from our Defense Attaché. To my way of thinking, the Pentagon erred in judgment because having the Air Force transport the bonsai would have gone a long way towards improving the status of our military in Japan.

BONSAI PRESENTATION CEREMONY IN COMMEMORATION OF THE U. S. BI-CENTENNIAL

5 *When faced with a similar situation during the nineteenth century, our Navy was very accommodating when it came to bringing plants from foreign shores. All naval vessels were instructed to gather and bring home new plants from ports of call. In 1853, the Navy actually outfitted its sailing ship, the* USS Release, *specifically to travel to South America to collect cuttings of sugarcane and she brought back 1,000 cases to New Orleans.*

A Pan Am Purchase Order

Until this moment, I had not had the courage to tell our Japanese friends the transportation was in dire peril. Fortunately, after the Air Force declined our request to fly the bonsai to their new home, the USDA issued a purchase order to Pan American Airlines to transport the bonsai from Japan. In reality, Pan American Airlines was a more experienced carrier in handling such unusual shipments.

The estimated cost of the purchase order ($2,340) seemed unrealistic but it was an encouraging start. We had no estimate of the size of the individual trees or the manner of packing. Further, we had no plans as to who would accompany the trees and certainly were not aware of the many official requirements that would be faced. We were to learn that one just does not fly off with a valuable collection like this, particularly when the Imperial Household is involved.

Then another problem arose. The Japanese side and the American Embassy wanted me to attend the presentation station ceremony on March 20. But my agency had a system of approved travel plans and if your plan was not on the list there was no chance to be included. The only solution was a strange one. Skip March had access to employee dependent travel because his wife was an airline employee. We decided that he would fly to Japan in my place at no cost to the U.S. government. I so advised the Nippon Bonsai Association and the American Embassy that March would attend the ceremony on behalf of the National Arboretum. Our good friend Dr. Frank Cullinan, the former chief of the USDA's Bureau of Plant and Industry and then a trustee of the Friends of the National Arboretum, agreed to pick up Skip's other expenses as the trip could not be funded by the agency.

Above Prince Takamatsu's Trident Maple (*Acer buergerianum*) shares a *tokonoma* with a Mountain Range Stone, one of six viewing stones included in the Bicentennial Gift.

Opposite Sylvester "Skip" March (left) and John Creech (right) with an unidentified man visit the Imperial Pine (*Pinus densiflora*) in the Imperial Household Collection.

I sent Mr. Edminster copies of the various letters about the ceremony and, all of a sudden, I was advised that the Agricultural Research Service was authorizing my travel. I immediately cabled our Embassy in Japan. Skip would still accompany me on the same financial arrangement as described above. We intended to return on the flight bringing the bonsai treasures to their new home. Without Skip's help, it would have been a most traumatic experience for me because there were so many details to be worked out in Japan.

Announcing the Gift

Meanwhile, plans for announcing the gift went forward—the ceremony would take place at the fabulous Hotel New Otani in Tokyo on March 20, 1975. I drafted a letter for Secretary of Agriculture Earl Butz to Dr. Henry Kissinger, then head of the National Security Council, describing this remarkable gift in honor of our Bicentennial, and equating it to the gift of flowering cherries by the Japanese. The USDA also issued a glowing press release. The American Embassy in Tokyo did its share, advising the Secretary of State of the gift and describing the involvement by both the Japanese government and Imperial Household. Full press coverage was planned for the presentation by former Prime Minister Nobusuke Kishi, the acceptance by Ambassador James D. Hodgson and my brief remarks. The ceremony in Japan was to be a major diplomatic affair. I thought it might be appropriate to present the Japanese with a silver Bicentennial commission medal that Congress had authorized, and I persuaded the Commission to give me one to take to Japan.

Bringing the Gift to the United States

Ceremony in Tokyo

By early 1975, preparations were completed to receive the bonsai collection at the Glenn Dale station, where the plants would be placed into quarantine. Two greenhouse sections had been emptied of other plants, and the benches had been sterilized and filled with clean gravel. Bob Drechsler transferred his office from the National Arboretum to Glenn Dale.

With everything in readiness, Skip and I took off for Japan, arriving on March 19, 1975. Mr. Koide and a delegation of NBA directors, representatives of the American Embassy, Miss Junko Arima as interpreter, as well as some Japanese reporters, met us when Pan Am Flight 1 arrived at Haneda Airport in the late afternoon. After expressions of congratulations, I was prepared for Mr. Koide's first question: Was the Air Force going to transport the plants? When I replied that arrangements with the Air Force had fallen through, Mr. Koide exclaimed after a deep

breath, "Saaaaa," which in Japan is a note of serious despair. But I quickly said that we had arranged with Pan American Airlines to transport the plants and that this was probably a better idea. Much relieved, Mr. Koide said we must go immediately to the headquarters of the Nippon Bonsai Association to see the grooming of the plants for the grand presentation of the bonsai to the American people on the 20th. Of course with little sleep, we were not exactly prepared for this.

When Skip and I saw the size of some of the bonsai, we were aghast! In the Nippon Bonsai Association's courtyard, on several long tables, there were the bonsai to be presented—including many very large ones. We were duly impressed with the

activities of the magnificence of the bonsai, but uppermost in our minds was the question of how we were going to stretch $2,300 to pay the cost of shipping. And where would Pan Am find the space to accommodate such large bonsai safely? That night, neither of us had much sleep, wondering how we were going to resolve these problems. The next morning we immediately spoke to the Pan Am representative, Mr. Malcolm MacDonald, who said he could provide us with a cargo plane to handle the bonsai, but made clear that the cost would exceed our $2,300 budget.

Meanwhile, the day was spent getting ready for the festivities that were to take place in the afternoon of March 20. The guest list was most impressive. On

the American side, Ambassador Hodgson led the delegation which included all upper-level Embassy staff, separate U.S. departmental agencies, the American Chamber of Commerce, the major newspapers and airline officials. In all, the number was about 100 persons. There were naturally far more Japanese. Among them were four former prime ministers, members of the Diet from both conservative and liberal parties, departmental heads, representatives of the Japan Foundation and, of course, a large delegation consisting of members of the Nippon Bonsai Association and the donors of the bonsai. Many from the foreign community were also included as permitted. It was said that this was one of the few occasions when leaders of the opposition parties of the Diet appeared on the same stage together.

The ceremony opened promptly on time and

the band of the Imperial Household performed throughout the ceremony. The fifty bonsai and the six precious stones selected by the NBA were displayed around the perimeter of the main hall of the New Otani Hotel. The president of the NBA, Mr. Kishi, greeted the audience and Mr. Teisuka Takahashi, Vice President of the NBA, gave the opening remarks. He described how the bonsai had been selected from all four major islands of Japan, that they were "so noble as to reflect the real heart of the Japanese people" and that the bonsai would "serve as a Green Peace Mission to open a new road in the friendly cultural relations between the two nations." Ambassador Hodgson officially accepted the bonsai on behalf of the people of the United States. He assured the Japanese people that we would do our best to preserve, protect and promote their beauty and an understanding of their artistry among our

citizens in the coming years. He also likened the gift to that of the flowering cherries so many years before. I reiterated these viewpoints in my short speech, assuring the Japanese that these enduring symbols of our love of nature will be viewed by millions of Americans in the years to come.

Ambassador Hodgson then presented the Bicentennial Silver medal to former Prime Minister Kishi as a token of remembrance of the occasion. The guests then were invited to view the bonsai and partake of the refreshments. There were several toasts first with saké for the well-being of the plants in their future home at the U.S. National Arboretum, more informal speeches and then the guests mingled with the plants for the next several hours. "Fabulous" is the only way to describe the presentation, and I could not imagine the cost of the arrangements which were funded by the Japanese government.

Far left Sylvester "Skip" March inspecting the filler used to soften the impact of the crates' movements for the Bicentennial Gift bonsai shipment from Tokyo to Washington.

Left Members of the Nippon Bonsai Association waving goodbye to "their precious children" when the crated bonsai left their headquarters on March 31, 1975.

Left Dr. John Creech examining the crated Imperial Pine (*Pinus densiflora*) before it was loaded on a Pan Am 707 freighter for the flight to San Francisco.

Preparing the Gifts for Shipment

Immediately after the ceremony, the bonsai were returned to the NBA display yard in preparation for packing. This was an enormous task. The plants were spaced on display tables for preparation, and many members of the NBA were assigned to specific tasks for each plant. I got the impression that everyone wanted to share in the preparation of this important gift to the American people. First, each plant was repotted with a uniform soil mixture. Japanese plant quarantine officers meticulously examined the bonsai to assure that they would pass inspection by U.S. quarantine officials once they reached the United States. The soil surface of each pot was covered with cheesecloth, and then a layer of moist sphagnum moss, all of which was wrapped with bubble plastic sheeting and bound tightly with tape. The freshly repotted bonsai were then secured with cord to their pots.

Next, the crating began, the cost of which was borne by the Japanese government. Carpenters constructed individual crates on the spot to meet the size of each individual tree. These were sufficiently large to assure that no branches would touch the crate and yet would still fit through the door of a Pan Am 707 aircraft. An agent from the airline was there to check on this requirement. These cases were beautifully and meticulously crafted, consisting of a wooden base to which three slatted sides were attached. There was a false, thin plywood bottom stuffed underneath with shredded foam plastic and each plant rested on this, allowing for flexibility when the plane landed. The trees were placed in their individual cages and additionally secured with more lashings. After a final inspection by the quarantine people, the slatted fourth side and top sections were nailed in place. The suiseki stones were wrapped in heavy bubble plastic and crated similarly.

The crating operation required several days. During this time, Skip and I took care of the voluminous paperwork, including both Japanese and U.S. customs' documents, export licenses, quarantine certificates and airline manifests. There was even a document of consignment from the Imperial Household that I had to sign. When I looked at one customs' declaration the value of the 53 trees and six stones was listed as ¥131,100,000.

While the crating was going on, we learned which tree had been selected to be donated by the Imperial Household, and we were invited to the palace to see the choice. It was a 180-year-old red pine in a Chinese container that was of considerable historic importance. It stood about 5 feet tall and required four men to lift the pot.

By now we were in a state of real anxiety as to how I would explain to the Department of

Left The bonsai arrive in Glenn Dale, Maryland on April 1, 1975, and begin their quarantine period before the official dedication in July 1976.

Agriculture that the $2,300 authorization had to be parlayed into a considerably larger sum. Each time that the PAA agent told me the price was going up, I telephoned the Department and advised them, for something like $9,000 and again around $13,000. But, when we saw the size of the Emperor's bonsai and realized the size of the crate it would require, I threw all caution to the wind. I sent a letter to Mr. Edminister accepting full responsibility for the overrun. As it turned out the shipment would require an entire 707 freighter. I had just rented an aircraft for slightly over $19,000!

Pan American Airlines was especially generous, and their agent informed me that they were only billing for the cost to fly the aircraft to the U.S. Still, I had broken every rule in the bureaucratic book and did not know what to expect when I returned home to explain the overrun. Mentally I was prepared for the worst.

The Flight Home

With all trees crated, we were ready to fly home on March 31, 1975. The crated bonsai were loaded in seven trucks and lined up at the NBA headquarters. The NBA directors stood in a small group and, as the last truck rounded the corner, they became very quiet. I remember to this day their touching waves of goodbye to their precious children. This was a solemn moment for them as they were very anxious about the future of their magnificent bonsai.

It was late afternoon when Skip and I arrived at the Pan Am terminal at Haneda Airport. This was an exciting time for us as we watched the crates lifted onto pallets and then hoisted with a crane up to the loading dock of the freighter. It was late evening by the time all 59 crates were on board PAA flight 876 and the aircraft was ready to depart. Skip and I were listed as couriers on the manifest because the crew did not know what else to do with

us. We climbed the stairs into the flight deck and were greeted by the crew who informed us that there were no accommodations on freighters except for them. They motioned for us to go back to the freight compartment of the aircraft. There all we could see was crate after crate lined up the entire length of the plane. We did find two jump seats against the bulkhead and a large microwave oven for heating the crew's food. We strapped into the jump seats, the jets whined and off we headed for San Francisco.

There was, of course, no comfortable place to sleep and we were both dog-tired. We were given several blankets and found a place to lie down beside the crate containing the large wisteria bonsai. So we crawled under the blankets and eventually slept until we were awakened by a crew member as we approached the California coast just about dawn.

When the plane landed in San Francisco, we were met by Customs, Pan-American Airlines and USDA agents. The Agricultural inspector was especially helpful and assisted us through quarantine quickly. The Customs agent, however, had a problem. It seemed that USDA research materials were entered duty-free but nobody had envisioned that it would include a shipment of such high monetary value. Thankfully, he signed the release and said that the folks at our final Baltimore destination could solve the problem. We also insisted on clearance then so as to avoid delays in Baltimore. So on the form was written "State Department Letter to Follow," but I do not think one ever came.

Because Pan-American Airlines could not fly across the country, their agent in Tokyo had arranged for two United Airlines DC-8 cargo aircraft to transport the trees to Baltimore and they were standing by. The trees were transshipped. Skip took one plane and I the other, and off we went on the last leg of the journey. Our only concern was that the planes made a stop in Chicago to unload other freight, and we feared that if the crates were unloaded in the freezing weather the plants would be harmed. The Japanese maples were already coming into leaf. But the crews worked it out so that while the plane sat on the ground the trees were kept inside. We departed Chicago quickly and arrived at Baltimore International Airport on the evening of March 31. The plants were unloaded and put into a hanger until our trucks from the Glenn Dale station could take them to their new home. Skip and I were so tired we took a room at the nearby motel and slept until early the next morning.

The greenhouses at Glenn Dale were ready. Bob Drechsler and others from Glenn Dale and the National Arboretum were on hand when the trucks were unloaded and the crates placed on the ground outside the greenhouses. The trees were gently lifted out of the crates and taken into their new quarters. They were now Bob Drechsler's charges and he hovered over them like a hen over new-born chicks. The Japanese bonsai gift to the American people had arrived!

Making the Best of Quarantine

With the bonsai collection safely at Glenn Dale and Drechsler as the curator, he and the Glenn Dale staff proceeded to provide improved quarters for the trees. New insect screening was installed on the greenhouse windows and vents, attractive wooden slats were placed on the benches to avoid scratching the ceramic pots, and the entire greenhouse was thoroughly cleaned.

A few days after the collection arrived, John Naka came from California and walked through the collection giving suggestions to Bob. John pointed out that several of the "jins" (dead branches retained on the trees) needed treatment with lime-sulfur to intensify their whiteness. Bob obtained the lime-sulfur and painted the "jins" which promptly turned them yellow-orange. Being new at caring for bonsai, Bob was horrified at the color. But after a few days, the "jins" turned snowy white as they should be. Relief!

The presence of this splendid present from the Japanese people had a remarkable impact on the Department of Agriculture. Mr. Edminster was able to find funding for the cost of the transportation, and I did not "fall from grace" or go into debt personally. Probably the reason was that the collection was receiving considerable praise in the Washington press. The visits to Glenn Dale by Ambassador Fumihiko Togo and the entire senior staff of the Japanese Embassy doubtlessly helped as well....

A small delegation of Nippon Bonsai Association directors flew over from Japan in May to determine the health of the collection, and they were totally pleased with the way Bob was handling his new assignment. Everyone's main concern was whether the bonsai would tolerate quarantine greenhouse conditions during the summer. The extremely fine screening that was required for quarantine purposes cut down on air movement and resulted in higher temperatures. We had installed cooling fans in the greenhouse as a temporary measure, but that was not adequate. Fortunately, there was an unused screenhouse structure on the grounds that had been used to house quarantined citrus plant introductions. It made a perfect summer house. It had a glass-paned roof and screened sides. Furthermore, it was enclosed

Left Dr. Creech unwraps a bonsai in quarantine where it would stay for more than a year before moving to the Arboretum to begin its public life in 1976.

with high chain-link fencing and locked gates that gave added security for the bonsai. The structure was completely refurbished, and by June the bonsai were in their new quarters where they remained until autumn. This was especially reassuring to the NBA directors, and they returned home prepared to make glowing reports to their members.

Meanwhile, the quarantine inspectors made periodic visits to Glenn Dale and gave the trees a thorough going over. Happily for us, the inspectors were perfectly satisfied as to the health of all the bonsai and could find no insect or disease problems. We had to be somewhat selective in accommodating visitors because Glenn Dale was still a quarantine station, which gave us a good excuse to limit visitation. However, many bonsai club members requested to see the collection and, of course, we accommodated them as best we could.

We considered having John Naka come from California to consult on a regular basis. Because of financial limitations, however, the care of the collection was left strictly in the hands of Bob and his new volunteer assistants, Dorothy Warren, Ruth Lamanna and Janet Lanman. These faithful women were Bob's constant helpers throughout his tenure and soon refer to themselves as his "grandmothers."

The health of the collection was good except for the cryptomeria forest that had been in questionable health when it was chosen. Our Japanese friends admitted that perhaps it should not have been included. Although a couple of the small trees in the forest had died, Bob managed to give his special attention to the rest and brought them to a healthy condition by the end of the year. The Japanese especially praised this effort because Mr. Eisaku Satō, a former Prime Minister and Counselor of the NBA, had donated that particular forest.

Creating the Japanese Bonsai Pavilion

In June 1975, we received bid invitations for the design of the viewing pavilion from 48 architectural firms. Because of the special nature of the facility, an understanding of Japanese display concepts and garden design was of prime importance. The nationally known architectural firm of Sasaki Associates of Watertown, Massachusetts, was selected to provide the design components and to supervise construction. Mr. Hideo Sasaki had a fine reputation and served on the Fine Arts Commission for the nation's capital. His associate, Masao (Mas) Kinoshita, was an authority on Japanese design concepts.

I had already selected the most logical site for the garden, just off the broad central plaza that faced the administration building. This location offered two advantages. It was readily accessible by foot from the administration building and offered a degree of security. It was also close to parking.

After several concept meetings with the Sasaki architects, we finally agreed on the present design. It included an entrance walk through a forest of cryptomeria trees that would be under-planted with Japanese woodland plants....

The entire facility would be walled and open to the sky above. An outside perimeter walk would circle the wall and lead to the handsome double metal gates at the entrance of the garden....

During the late summer of 1975, the Arboretum's

Right A U.S. Department of Agriculture inspector examining a Bicentennial Gift bonsai with a magnifying loupe, looking for insects or disease problems.

maintenance supervisor, Bill Scarborough, undertook the rough grading and removal of excess shrubs and trees. He had to operate a small front-end loader delicately in very tight spaces to avoid damage to the perimeter walls that were being simultaneously constructed. With the grading finished, the planting of the entrance trees could begin. Among the specimens that could now be planted were the 23 cryptomerias for the outside perimeter walk. Locating mature trees would be a considerable expense. Fortunately, Scarborough had previously worked for the well-known Greenbrier Farms Nursery and approached them with our need. We paid a visit to the nursery and were shown a field of abandoned cryptomeria trees, some of which were 20 or more feet tall. We were offered these for only the cost of transportation from middle Virginia.

It was the old transportation story all over again because one early morning in October several large trucks loaded with the balled cryptomerias appeared at the Arboretum. I had not even contracted for them and the bill was several thousand dollars. But again our business office at Beltsville, Maryland, managed to work out details and my reputation was again saved. With his skilled use of the loader, Scarborough smoothly placed these large trees in perfect alignment to make the pathway into the pavilion....

There was a need for a row of tall crapemyrtle trees set on mounds to permit their tops to appear above the wall. There was only one place to acquire them and that was from Donald Egolf, the Arboretum's famous crapemyrtle breeder. One had to know Don to realize that getting him to release some of his precious "children" for our cause would not be easy. After all, we had absconded with his top technician, Bob Drechsler. But when I approached him, Don generously offered some of the best hybrid

seedlings in his nursery. Today, these are a spectacular aspect of the entrance garden. What makes this more interesting is the fact that one parent of these hybrids is the rare *Lagerstroemia fauriei* that I had introduced from Japan back in 1956. So I suppose Don felt that he owed me something.

Now came the matter of stones befitting a Japanese garden. Mas Kinoshita was to personally select these for their individual character and, as many know, this is something only a trained Japanese eye can appreciate. So one cold snowy January day he and I drove to a stone quarry near Valley Forge, Pennsylvania, arriving late in the day to pick out the stones. As cold as it was, Mas moved easily among the candidate stones, selecting them for quality and

Above In summer, the trees were moved outside within the quarantine area. The Imperial Pine is the largest in this image and the Yamaki Pine is to its right.

character, and assuring that they had the proper faces and other aspects to meet his rigid standards. In Japan he could have gone to a "stone" nursery where choice stones are for sale, but his selections were both handsome and unblemished. How appropriate it was to have stones from Valley Forge for the Bicentennial garden. Upon delivery, Mas marked each stone's front and reserved it for its chosen location. With the help of Bill Scarborough, they each were placed at the correct depth in the standard Japanese manner using a pole tripod and ropes.

Development of a Logo

One item I considered important was a logo for the collection—that is, a kind of family crest (*mon*) such as I had so often seen in Japan. This would be a visual identity of the National Bonsai Collection. In February, I requested assistance from the USDA Visual Services, and Beverly Hoge of the USDA Office of Communication was assigned to locate a graphic arts specialist to effect the design. I suggested that the crest be designed within a circle similar to those depicted in the Japanese book of crests, and I loaned my copy to Ms. Hoge for guidance.

A local graphics designer, Ann Masters, accepted the contract to develop the concept that ultimately became the symbol of the entire bonsai and penjing complex. This design was later adopted as the symbol of the support organization, the National Bonsai Foundation. Ms. Masters had traveled in Japan and had freelanced for several prominent magazines, including Time/Life. The concept was to be drawn from the collection itself, and she provided several sketches using various stylized versions.

Ms. Masters visited the collection at Glenn Dale and chose the 250-year-old Shimpaku (*Juniperus chinensis*, var. *sargentii)*. Her initial sketches consisted of a Juniper with the twisted trunk and masses of foliage to depict the luxurious growth of the collection. The final design featured the Juniper within a double circle, reflecting the sturdiness of the bonsai tree and its massive foliage. Because a branch broke the bands of the circle, the design also symbolized the continued vigor of the trees in their new home.

Left The National Bonsai & Penjing Museum's logo is emblazoned on one of its gates, with the U.S. National Arboretum's Capitol Columns seen in the distance.

Above The Sargent Juniper (*Juniperus chinensis* var. *sargentii*), whose twisted trunk and pyramid-shaped foliage inspired the logo design, shown with its donor, Mr. Kenichi Oguchi.

Above right Tsunekazu Nakajima, a Nippon Bonsai Association member, makes final adjustments to the logo tree in preparation for the dedication ceremony in 1976.

Below right A sequence of sketches demonstrates the development of the museum's logo created by Ann Masters along the lines of a Japanese family crest or *mon*.

The NBA Directors Visit Their Bonsai

In October 1975, a large delegation of NBA directors traveled to Washington to see how the bonsai were doing. As this was the first visit to the United States for most of them, we planned a gala event. First and foremost was a visit to Glenn Dale to see the collection and hold discussions with Bob Drechsler and his volunteer assistants, Ruth Lamanna and Janet Lanman, both longtime bonsai growers and members of the Potomac Bonsai Association. Mas Kinoshita was also present along with Skip March and me so that we could discuss the plans for the viewing pavilion at the Arboretum. It was important that Kinoshita be present because he could discuss the plan in Japanese since these elderly bonsai masters spoke little English and depended on the young interpreter for other conversations.

The NBA directors were delighted with the health of the bonsai. They made a few observations on training and maintenance to Bob, and said some of the plants never looked better. Then they were taken to the deep pit greenhouse where the plants could over-winter. This was an unheated pit greenhouse dug in English style several feet below the ground surface and completely frost proof. This especially pleased the visitors. The next few days we escorted them to sites around Washington, including a visit to Mount Vernon, a private visit to the White House, and a trip to Longwood Gardens in Kennett Square, Pennsylvania.

The last of their four-day visit ended up at the Arboretum where they inspected the pavilion site that was then only a graded area. But they saw all

Left Two directors from the Nippon Bonsai Association, Hideo Chugun and Nobukichi Koide, inspect the bonsai in quarantine in Glenn Dale, Maryland.

the plans and held further discussions, particularly with Mas Kinoshita, and were greatly pleased when we explained that everything was aimed at a July 9, 1976 dedication. As they were leaving for the airport, one of the directors stated that they would like to present 20 additional bonsai to complete the collection. While I expressed appreciation for the offer, in my mind I had enough on my plate for the present and let the matter rest until I heard further from Japan. But just to set the opportunity in motion, I wrote to our plant quarantine colleague, Ivan Rainwater, about the offer and received a letter of authorization for future importation. This did not actually occur until 1998, so the Japanese do have long memories.

The NBA directors brought with them a 16 mm film that they called "How the Bonsai Came to America," which captured the entire sequence of events in Japan earlier in the year. This documentary was shown at the Arboretum many times that autumn, including to Ambassador and Madame Togo on the occasion of their visit to the Arboretum and Glenn Dale. We had become fast friends with the Japanese Embassy staff and on several occasions Skip March and I were invited to receptions at the Embassy. Skip was often asked for advice on plantings at the new embassy residence. In addition to the film, the NBA produced a beautiful folio size documentary book in English on the presentation ceremony with full-page photographs of each of the bonsai and stones in the collection and the text of each of the speeches that were made. These books have become an historic record of the Japanese side of the gift and were presented to various American officials and agencies concerned with the occasion.

The Dedication Ceremony

As January 1976 arrived, construction of the pavilion and the entrance garden was moving forward on schedule. The bonsai were now safe in their winter quarters in the deep pit greenhouse and would require minimum care for the next few months.

But there was considerable planning yet to be done in preparation for the dedication ceremony. Skip March was in charge of planning the effort to present a typical Japanese bonsai show with its elegant bunting, lanterns and other regalia. Meanwhile, Bob Drechsler was in regular communication with the NBA concerning the timing for the movement of the plants from winter quarters back to the screen house and the spring pruning activities. I turned my attention to the several official arrangements for the dedication of the pavilion and the bonsai presentation to the American public.

The Secretary of Agriculture, Earl L. Butz, was especially supportive of our plans, and the USDA arranged for 2,000 formal invitations to be printed. These were to be sent to members of the bonsai community, local garden club members (who were always a great help to the Arboretum), various government and other local officials, the press, anyone else who had heard of the affair and, of course, all the Arboretum staff who had worked so wonderfully to meet our dateline. In addition, we sent invitations to the directors of the NBA in Japan and were almost caught off guard, not realizing that by inviting them they might expect that we would pay the transportation and other expenses. However, our good friends at the American Embassy in Japan

Left Bamboo slats provided shade and created distinctive shadows when the Japanese Pavilion was new in 1976.

Below Members of the Toho Koto Society of Washington, D.C., entertained guests at the Dedication Ceremony by playing traditional songs on *koto*, stringed instruments known as the national instrument of Japan.

nipped this in the bud by explaining that governmental funds could not be so used. But they all came anyway.

The next item was planning the program speakers. We asked Ambassador Togo to make a presentation; Mr. Koide would present the collection to the American people; and Secretary Butz had agreed to say a few words. For the principal speaker, we turned to our loyal friend Dr. Henry Kissinger, who had been kept apprised of the progress over the past two years. He graciously consented to be the main

speaker even though he already had a formal engagement later that evening.

Meanwhile, Skip March requested bunting (*taremaku*), bonsai turntables, Japanese watering cans and other accessories from the NBA that are commonly found in Japanese bonsai gardens. An American bonsai and suiseki enthusiast in Tokyo, Mr. Donald Sanborn, agreed to provide Japanese lanterns and umbrellas. All of these materials were sent to us by the embassy's diplomatic pouch, thus avoiding customs difficulties. Throughout this entire

saga, our friends at the American Embassy in Tokyo bore much of the communication burden as well as making so many important arrangements in dealing with the Japanese government and Imperial Household. We had asked that our closest contact at the American Embassy, Mr. Takeo Takeshita, be given travel orders to come to Washington for the dedication and this request was granted. In addition, our dear friend Kaname Kato, who was so instrumental in getting the entire project underway, and his wife also planned to attend the dedication ceremony.

In June 1976, the tension was mounting. Four directors of the NBA arrived a couple of days before the dedication ceremony to assist Bob Drechsler in the final grooming of the bonsai and to lend their expertise in the placement of the trees on the staging that was arranged around the Arboretum's plaza. Skip concentrated on the decorations, the final manicuring of the entrance garden and the coordination of the various activities with the garden clubs. The Arboretum's lead secretary, Mrs. Doris Thibodo, sent out the invitations. By July 9, all was in readiness.

Left For the Dedication Ceremony, some bonsai were shown on the terrace adjacent to the U.S. National Arboretum's administration building, pool and fountain.

Opposite left Secretary of State Henry Kissinger spoke to nearly 2,000 people at the Dedication Ceremony. Japanese Speaker of the House Kenzo Kono and Japanese Ambassador Fumihiko Togo flank his empty chair.

Opposite right Secretary of State Kissinger, with Creech at his side, autographed copies of the Dedication Ceremony's program with the museum's logo on its cover.

The Gods Smile on Us

It seemed that nothing could tarnish this historic event. The attendance was now expected to approach 2,000 guests and it seemed that everyone in Washington of some importance wanted to be present. The festivities were to begin at 7:00 p.m. with initial remarks by Secretary Butz, Ambassador Togo and Mr. Koide. Secretary of State Kissinger was to be the featured speaker at 7:30 p.m.

Strange events always arise that seem to mar a perfect plan. During the day prior to the ceremony, I received a telephone call from the customs people at Dulles international Airport. There was a large Japanese screen waiting to be released as soon as a bill of some several hundred dollars was paid. Of course, I could not agree to pay such an unknown charge with Arboretum funds and initially thought we would have to reject the screen.

In conversations with the State Department, however, I learned that the donor of the screen, Mr. Tinkei Tachibana, was a very important person with connections to the Imperial family, and to reject the screen would have been an embarrassment to Japan and U.S. relations. Realizing this, and with the help from the Japan-America Society of Washington, the Japan Society of New York and the Friends of the National Arboretum, we rescued the screen. It was

Left Masaru Yamaki, donor of a Japanese White Pine (*Pinus parviflora* 'Miyajima'), which had been in his family since 1625, was delighted to find the tree thriving.

a gigantic, heavily gold-embossed affair with a large red sign and an impression of the Imperial red pine in the background. It weighed several hundred pounds, which accounted for the excessive shipping costs. We were advised that Mr. Tachibana was planning to visit the day after the dedication and it was important for the screen to be displayed.

There was perfect weather on July 9, 1976 for the dedication and everything was in order early in the afternoon. By 7:00 p.m. the guests began arriving. Tight security was furnished by the District of Columbia police and their federal counterparts. The Marine Corps Band began to play lively tunes, and we were entertained by the members of the Washington Toho Koto society, dressed in Japanese costumes. I escorted Secretary Kissinger, Ambassador

Togo, Secretary Butz and their wives on a tour of the bonsai display. Secretary Kissinger's fine speech emphasized the good relations between Japan and the United States. He highly praised the Japanese for their most exceptional gift, as he was aware of the significance of bonsai in Japanese culture, emphasizing that there bonsai would find a similar appreciation in their new home. The gates to the bonsai pavilion were opened so that both the Japanese and American guests might stroll through the entrance garden and mingle while enjoying a lovely evening for the next three hours. A full moon and the Japanese lanterns Skip had placed in the trees surrounding the pavilion made a delightful scene. As Mr. Koide remarked to me, "the gods must have smiled on us." It was a perfect evening.

The next day the pavilion was open to the public. There was extensive press coverage. Both local and national newspapers such as the *Washington Star* and the *New York Times* provided feature articles with terms like "small is beautiful" and "bonsai bansai." Over the next several days congratulatory letters poured into Secretary Butz's office and they were passed on to me.

Bob Drechsler and his assistants, Ruth Lamanna and Janet Lanman, were now in complete charge of their legacy. A steady stream of visitors, including some from Japan, viewed the collection during the next several months. It was a dramatic moment when Mr. Masaru Yamaki, who donated the 350-year-old white pine, stood in front of his tree with tears in his eyes and observed that this is how he always wanted his tree to look.

In March 2001, Mr. Yamaki's two grandsons visited the National Arboretum to see their grandfather's white pine. While admiring this great bonsai, they explained to Curator Warren Hill that during World War II their grandfather's nursery was in Hiroshima and that this white pine had survived the bombing of that city because it was behind a wall even though merely three km from the blast.

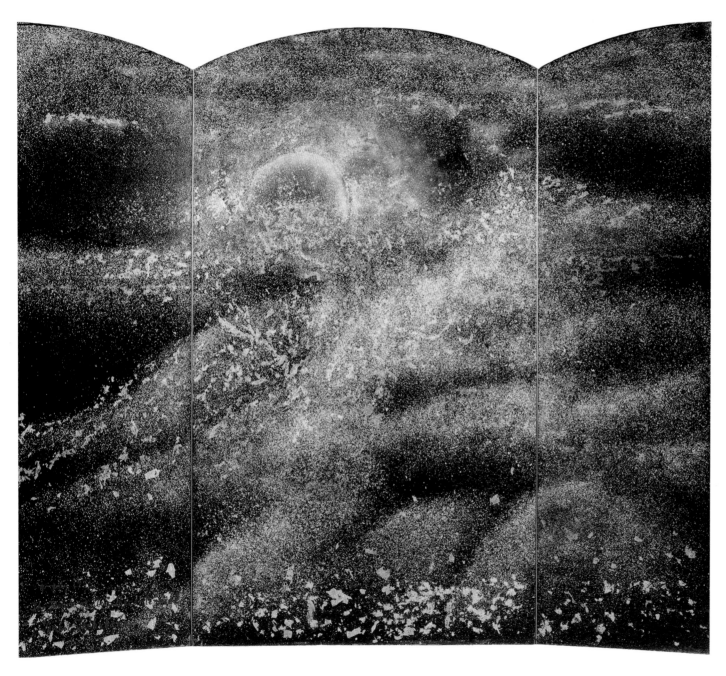

Left A splendid gold-embossed screen with a large red sun and an impression of the Imperial Pine was a surprise additional gift from a Japanese donor.

Right The National Bonsai &
Penjing Museum includes both
open and covered spaces,
complemented by gardens and
courtyards, encouraging visitors to
linger and enjoy nature's beauty.

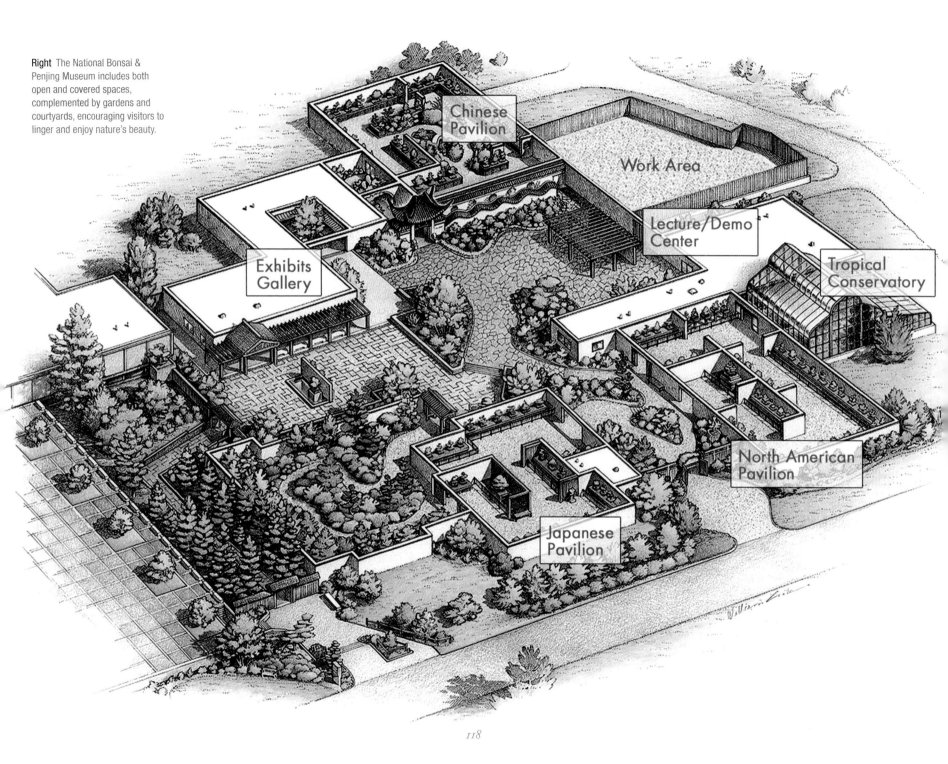

Chinese
Pavilion

Work Area

Lecture/Demo
Center

Exhibits
Gallery

Tropical
Conservatory

North American
Pavilion

Japanese
Pavilion

Endnote

Well, this is the story of how the Bicentennial bonsai collection came to America. The drama continues to the present day under the direction of more recent National Arboretum directors and the wonderful leadership and financial support of the National Bonsai Foundation.

Bob Drechsler continued to care for his charges in a most dedicated fashion until his retirement in 1996. It is indicative of Bob's sensitivity for the bonsai collection that he considered his main objective throughout his career to maintain the integrity of each tree as originally styled. He kept a small notebook with a sketch of each tree. This reference became "dog eared" from constant referral by the time he retired.

What began as a modest idea for having a small collection of bonsai at the National Arboretum has resulted in the creation of the National Bonsai & Penjing Museum, with over 150 masterpiece bonsai and penjing in Japanese, Chinese and American collections. Without question, the Bicentennial gift of Japanese bonsai has been the most important role played by plants in furthering the diplomatic relationship between Japan and the United States since the presentation of the flowering cherries at the beginning of the twentieth century. This gift has helped turn the art of bonsai from a mainly Japanese tradition into an international activity with bonsai artists throughout the world.

I am sure that many of these miniature trees in the Japanese Collection will be living witnesses to the enduring friendship between the United States and Japan during the next Centennial celebration at the National Arboretum.

John Creech

Above John Creech with the Bicentennial Gift trees in quarantine, next to the Sargent Juniper (*Juniperus chinensis* var. *sargentii*) that inspired the logo.

Spotlight on the Museum Curators

The fine care that the trees in the collections of the National Bonsai & Penjing Museum receive, their artful presentation, and the Museum's educational outreach activities are all under the purview of the curator. The museum and its collections have been fortunate in the individuals who have served as curator since 1975.

Robert "Bonsai Bob" Drechsler was the founding curator, serving in that capacity for more than twenty years, from 1975 to 1996. Ably assisted by the late Dan Chiplis, Drechsler set the high standards for the care of the collection that are still maintained today.

Warren Hill succeeded him, serving from 1996 to 2001. Jack Sustic followed Hill, from 2002 to 2005, and was succeeded by Jim Hughes, from 2005 to 2008. Jack Sustic returned to the curatorship in 2008 to the present.

Curators, of course, do not work alone. A large part of the museum's success is also due to its committed staff, volunteers and interns, all of whom work in tandem with the curator, caring for each small tree or tiny landscape in the museum.

Warren Hill

Robert "Bonsai Bob" Drechsler with Dan Chiplis

Jack Sustic

Jim Hughes

Michael James

The National Bonsai & Penjing Museum Honorees

Since its opening in 1976, the National Bonsai & Penjing Museum has attracted interest and support from bonsai enthusiasts and practitioners as well as from the general public. Some of its most significant supporters are remembered by specific museum spaces. The North American Pavilion is dedicated to John Y. Naka, the Tropical Conservatory to Haruo "Papa" Kaneshiro, the Chinese Pavilion to Dr. Yee-Sun Wu and the Educational Center to Yuji Yoshimura. The Kato Family Stroll Garden recognizes Saburo Kato's profound contributions, while the garden of North American native plants at the museum's exit honors George Yamaguchi.

Other features recall important museum benefactors. Maria Rivera Vanzant, who with her husband Howard was an ardent bonsai enthusiast, is remembered in the Upper Courtyard. The H. William Merritt Gate honors a volunteer and National Bonsai Foundation member who built the *tokonoma* display area himself. The Exhibit Gallery is dedicated to Mary E. Mrose, a mineralogist, crystallographer and bonsai aficionado who believed that bonsai, penjing and viewing stones deserve serious study. The Melba Tucker Arbor honors the author of *Suiseki & Viewing Stones, an American Perspective* for her exemplary service to bonsai and its related art forms in California and beyond. The Rose Family Garden, encircling the Lower Courtyard, recognizes the significant contributions of Deborah Rose, especially in support of the Japanese Pavilion renovation. Barbara Hall Marshall has supported the National Bonsai & Penjing Museum and the National Bonsai Foundation in innumerable ways and is the major benefactor of the John Y. Naka Pavilion. Another devoted patron is Marybel Balendonck, friend and student of John Naka, who is the primary advocate for the museum on the west coast.

The National Bonsai & Penjing Museum and the National Bonsai Foundation thank all those whose commitment and contributions of every kind make the museum and its collections such a unique and special place in the nation's capital and in the world.

Haruo "Papa" Kaneshiro, Tropical Conservatory dedication, 1993

Melba Tucker, 1988

Barbara Hall Marshall
and Marybel Balendonck, 2009

Left to right: Robert Drechsler, Dr. Thomas Elias, Mary E. Mrose,
Floyd Horn and Mary Ann Orlando, Exhibits Gallery dedication, 1996

Saburo Kato with *The Remotest Hill*, his first forest planting of Ezo spruce trees, in Omiya, Japan

Deborah Rose and Harry Hirao, 2011

George Yamaguchi, North American Garden dedication, 1993

Left to right: Mary Ann Orlando, H. William Merritt and John Y. Naka, North American Pavilion groundbreaking, 1988

Left to right: Yuji Yoshimura, John Y. Naka, Dr. Henry Marc Cathey and Frederic Ballard, North American Pavilion groundbreaking, 1988

Maria Rivera Vanzant and Vaughn Banting, Lake Charles Bonsai Society, 1991

Select Bonsai Collections in North America

Below In training since 1978, this Satsuki evergreen azalea "Gunbo-nishiki" was created by the museum's first curator, Robert "Bonsai Bob" Drechsler.

Weyerhaeuser Bonsai Garden, Garvan Woodland Gardens, Hot Springs National Park, Arkansas

The Huntington, San Marino, California

Safari Park Bonsai Pavilion, San Diego Wild Animal Park, California

The Golden State Bonsai Federation, The Huntington, San Marino, California

The Golden State Bonsai Federation, Lake Merritt, Oakland, California

The Golden State Bonsai Federation, Clark Center Bonsai Collection, Fresno, California

Denver Botanic Gardens, Denver, Colorado

U.S. National Arboretum, Washington, D.C.

Heathcote Botanical Gardens, Fort Pierce, Florida

Morikami Museum and Japanese Gardens, Delray Beach, Florida

Chicago Botanic Garden, Glencoe, Illinois

The Arnold Arboretum, Boston, Massachusetts

Matthaei Botanical Gardens and Nichols Arboretum, Ann Arbor, Michigan

The Richard & Helen DeVos Japanese Garden at Frederik Meijer Gardens & Sculpture Park, Grand Rapids, Michigan

The Charlotte Partridge Ordway Japanese Garden, Como Park Zoo & Conservatory, St. Paul, Minnesota

North Carolina Arboretum, Asheville, North Carolina

Brooklyn Botanic Garden, Brooklyn, New York

Longwood Gardens, Kennett Square, Pennsylvania

Phipps Conservatory, Pittsburgh, Pennsylvania

Pacific Bonsai Museum, Federal Way, Washington

Dr. Sun Yat-Sen Classical Chinese Garden, Vancouver, British Columbia, Canada

Montréal Botanical Garden, Montréal, Québec, Canada

Bibliography

Albek, Morten with Wayne Schoech, *Majesty in Miniature, Shohin Bonsai, Unlocking the Secrets of Small Trees*. Passumpsic, Vermont: Stone Lantern Publishing, 2007.

Albert, Karin, "Mountains and Water in Chinese Art." *Bonsai Clubs International*, September/October 1988, Volume XXVII, No. 5.

_____, "Rocks and Rock Landscapes." *Bonsai Clubs International*, September/October 1988, Volume XXVII, No. 5.

Allinson, Mary, "A Short History of Tiny Trees." Longwood Gardens Blog, June 9, 2015.

Baran, Robert J., "Bonsai Book of Days." www.phoenixbonsai.com.

Becker, Rachel A., "This Bonsai Survived Hiroshima But Its Story Was Nearly Lost." news.nationalgeographic.com, August 5, 2015.

Bloomer, Mary Holmes with photographs by Peter L. Bloomer, *Timeless Trees, the U.S. National Bonsai Collection*. Flagstaff, Arizona: Horizons West, 1986.

Brown, Kendall H., *Quiet Beauty, The Japanese Gardens of North America*. Tokyo, Rutland, Vermont, Singapore: Tuttle Publishing, 2013.

_____, "Territories of Play: A Short History of Japanese-Style Gardens in North America." *Japanese-Style Gardens of the Pacific West Coast*, New York, Rizzoli, 1999.

Buchanan, Joy, "John Y. Naka, 89; Brought Art of Asian Bonsai to West." *Los Angeles Times*, May 24, 2004.

Cathey, Henry M., *Growing Bonsai*. Washington, D.C.: U.S. Department of Agriculture, Home and Garden Bulletin No. 206, 1977.

Chan, Peter, *Bonsai Secrets, Designing, Growing and Caring for Your Miniature Masterpiece*. Pleasantville, New York: The Reader's Digest Association, Inc., 2006.

Chester-Davis, Leah, "John L. Creech: A Giant in Plant Exploration." *The Trillium*, Vol. 24, Issue 2, March–April 2014.

_____, "The Horticultural Legacy of John L. Creech." YouTube Presentation, JC Raulston Arboretum, May 21, 2014.

Choukas-Bradley, Melanie, *City of Trees, The Complete Field Guide to the Trees of Washington, D.C.*, Charlottesville and London: The University Press of Virginia, 2008.

Clark, Randy T., *Outstanding American Bonsai*. Portland, Oregon: Timber Press, 1989.

Covello, Vincent T. and Yoshimura, Yuji, *The Japanese Art of Stone Appreciation, Suiseki and Its Use with Bonsai*. Tokyo, Rutland, Vermont, Singapore: Tuttle Publishing, 2009.

Creech, Dr. John, *The Bonsai Saga, How the Bicentennial Collection Came to America*. Washington, D.C.: The National Bonsai Foundation, 2001.

Crutcher, Anne, "Q and A, Devoting His Life's Work to Arboretum." *The Washington Star*, September 5, 1976.

Del Tredici, Peter, *Early American Bonsai: The Larz Anderson Collection of the Arnold Arboretum*. Jamaica Plain, Massachusetts: Arnold Arboretum of Harvard University, 1989.

_____, "The Larz Anderson Collection of Japanese Dwarf Trees and the Early Importation of 'Chabo Hiba' Hinoki Cypress into North America." Washington, D.C.: National Bonsai Foundation, *Proceedings of the International Scholarly Symposium on Bonsai and Viewing Stones*, May 2002.

Drechsler, Robert, telephone interview, July 13, 2015.

Durham, Sharon, "State Department's Gift of Dogwoods to Japan in Honor of 100th Anniversary of Cherry Tree Gift." *Agricultural Research*, February 2013.

Elias, Thomas S., "History of the Introduction and Establishment of Bonsai in the Western World." Washington, D.C.: National Bonsai Foundation, *Proceedings of the International Scholarly Symposium on Bonsai and Viewing Stones*, May 2002.

Elias, Thomas S. and Nakaoji, Hiromi, *Chrysanthemum Stones, The Story of Stone Flowers*. Warren, Connecticut: Floating World Editions, 2010.

Forgey, Benjamin, "Capitol's Columns Moved to Arboretum." *The Washington Post*, June 27, 1984.

Fukumoto, David W., "The Many Facets of Chinese Bonsai." *Bonsai Clubs International*, September/October 1988, Volume XXVII, No. 5.

Funk, Brian and Schmidt, Sarah (eds), *Japanese-Style Gardens*. Brooklyn, New York: Brooklyn Botanic Garden, 2015.

Gillette, Felix, "The Education of Little Trees, Day by Day, Twig by Twig, National Bonsai and Penjing Museum curator Warren Hill trains a remarkable collection of tiny timber." www.washingtoncitypaper.com, April 6, 2001.

Gustafson, Herb L., *Miniature Bonsai.* New York: Sterling Publishing Co. Inc., 1995.

Hammer, Elizabeth, *A Closer Look, Nature Within Walls, The Chinese Garden Court at the Metropolitan Museum of Art.* New York: The Metropolitan Museum of Art, 2003.

Helphand, Kenneth, *Defiant Gardens [online extension].* San Antonio: Trinity University Press, 2006.

Hinds, Colonel John, "National Bonsai Collection Begins." *The Bonsai Bulletin,* Vol.11, No. 4, Winter 1973.

Horton, Alvin, *Ortho's All About Creating Japanese Gardens.* Des Moines, Iowa: Meredith® Books, 2003.

House, Toni, "A Big, Little, Blooming Gift." *The Washington Star,* May 4, 1976.

Kato, Saburo, edited and compiled by William N. Valavanis, *Forest, Rock Planting & Ezo Spruce Bonsai.* Washington, D.C.: The National Bonsai Foundation, 2001.

Kawana, Dr. Koichi, "The Japanese Garden: A Reflection of Japanese Character, Part I." *Missouri Botanic Garden Bulletin,* 1975, Volume 63, No. 17.

_____, "The Japanese Garden: A Reflection of Japanese Character, Part II." *Missouri Botanic Garden Bulletin,* 1975, Volume 63, No. 18.

_____, "Symbolism and Esthetics in the Japanese Garden." *Missouri Botanic Garden Bulletin,* 1977, Volume 65, No. 6.

Kobayashi, Kunio and Tajima, Kazuhiko, *Bonsai.* Tokyo, Japan: PIE International, Inc., 2011.

Mahoney, Hal, "Chinese Rock Penjing, Emphasis on Construction." *Bonsai Clubs International,* September/October 1988, Volume XXVII, No. 5.

Marushima, Hideo, "History of Japanese Bonsai Appreciation." Washington, D.C.: National Bonsai Foundation, *Proceedings of the International Scholarly Symposium on Bonsai and Viewing Stones,* May 2002.

_____, "History of Japanese Suiseki." Washington, D.C.: National Bonsai Foundation, *Proceedings of the International Scholarly Symposium on Bonsai and Viewing Stones,* May 2002.

Matsuura, Arishige, "Japanese Suiseki." Washington, D.C.: National Bonsai Foundation, *Proceedings of the International Scholarly Symposium on Bonsai and Viewing Stones,* May 2002.

McArthur, Meher, *Reading Buddhist Art, An Illustrated Guide to Buddhist Signs & Symbols.* London: Thames & Hudson, 2002.

McNatt, Cindy, "Bonsai Master Harry Hirao." *Orange County Register,* December 7, 2013.

Morring, Frank Jr,. "Tiny Trees Pose Big Job for Keepers." *The New York Times,* September 11, 1988.

Mowry, Robert, "Chinese Scholars Rocks." Washington, D.C.: National Bonsai Foundation, *Proceedings of the International Scholarly Symposium on Bonsai and Viewing Stones,* May 2002.

Nakamura, Susumu and Watters, Ivan, *Bonsai, A Patient Art.* New Haven, Connecticut: Chicago Botanic Garden in association with Yale University Press, 2012.

North American Bonsai Federation Editorial Team, "A Tribute to John Naka." *North American Bonsai Federation,* Newsletter #1, November 2002.

Packard, Aarin, "Bonsai From The National Bonsai & Penjing Museum, Part 1: The Princess and The Tree." *International Bonsai,* No. 3, 2012.

Parsell, Diana, "Yokohama Nursery." www.agreatblooming.com, April 13, 2013.

Pearson, Lisa, "The Yokohama Nursery Company: Japanese Plants for Western Buyers." *Library Leaves,* **www.arboretum.harvard.edu**.

Peters, Gerhard and Woolley, John T., "Remarks of the President and King Hassan II of Morocco following their Meetings, May 19, 1982." *The American Presidency Project,* **http://www.presidency.ucsb.edu/ws/?pid=42539**.

Ragle, Larry, "The Stones of California." Washington, D.C.: National Bonsai Foundation, *Proceedings of the International Scholarly Symposium on Bonsai and Viewing Stones,* May 2002.

Ragle, Nina Shire, *Even Monkeys Fall Out of Trees, John Naka's Collection of Japanese Proverbs.* Laguna Beach, California: Nippon Art Forms, 1987.

Sawada, Ikune, "Notes on Antique Chinese Bonsai Pots." *Bonsai Clubs International,* September/October 1988, Volume XXVII, No. 5.

Saxon, Wolfgang, "Yuji Yoshimura, 76, a Master of the Ancient Art of Bonsai." *The New York Times,* January 4, 1998.

Siddiqui, Faiz, "Still growing strong, 70 years after atomic blast." *The Washington Post,* August 3, 2015.

Stowell, Jerald, "Bonsai as Living Sculpture." Washington, D.C.: National Bonsai Foundation, *Proceedings of the International Scholarly Symposium on Bonsai and Viewing Stones,* May 2002.

Taylor, Patrick, editor, *The Oxford Companion to the Garden.* Oxford: Oxford University Press, 2006.

The National Bonsai & Penjing Museum, *Awakening the Soul, The National Viewing Stone Collection.* Washington, D.C.: U.S. National Arboretum, 2000.

_____, *Beyond Wonderment and Curiosity*. Washington, D.C.: U.S. National Arboretum, 1990.

_____, *Bonsai Tours* app accessed in 2015.

_____, *Luxuriant Hothouse*. Washington, D.C.: U.S. National Arboretum, 1993.

_____, *What's Past is Prologue*. Washington, D.C.: U.S. National Arboretum, 1996.

The National Bonsai Foundation, Inc., *NBF Bulletin*. Winter 1998, volume X, number 2 to present.

The North American Bonsai Federation, *5th World Bonsai Convention, Bringing the World Together Through Bonsai*. Washington, D.C.: The North American Bonsai Federation, 2005.

Tierney, Professor Lennox, *The Nature of Japanese Garden Art*. San Diego: Japanese Friendship Garden, 1996.

Unknown Author, "Chapter 4: East Meets West in Balboa Park." San Diego History Center.

_____, "Definitions Helpful for Landscape Style Bonsai." Washington, D.C.: National Bonsai Foundation, *Proceedings of the International Scholarly Symposium on Bonsai and Viewing Stones, May 2002*.

_____, "Dr. Creech Honored." *Evening Star*, June 29, 1975.

_____, "Dr. Creech Wins Medal." *Evening Star*, September 28, 1969.

_____, *Kale's Tree and Shrub Reference Book, 2015*. Princeton, New Jersey: Kale's Nursery & Landscape Service, 2015.

Valavanis, William, "National Bonsai Hall of Fame." valavanisbonsaiblog.com, June 21, 2015.

_____, "Yuji Yoshimura, A Memorial Tribute to a Bonsai Master & Pioneer." *International Bonsai* 1998, No. 1.

Welch, Patricia Bjaaland, *Chinese Art, A Guide to Motifs and Visual Imagery*. Tokyo, Rutland, Vermont, Singapore: Tuttle Publishing, 2008.

Yoshimura, Yuji and Halford, Giovanna M., *The Art of Bonsai, Creation, Care, Enjoyment*. Rutland, Vermont: Tuttle Publishing, 1957.

Young, Dorothy S., *Bonsai, The Art and Technique*. Englewood Cliffs, New Jersey: Prentice-Hall, 1985.

Youngman, Wilbur H., "Creech Heads Arboretum." *The Sunday Star and Daily News*, April 1, 1973.

Yunhua, Hu, *Penjing, The Chinese Art of Miniature Gardens*. Beaverton, Oregon: Timber Press, 1982.

Zhao, Qingquan, *Literati Style Penjing, Chinese Bonsai Masterworks*. New York, NY: Better Link Press, 2015.

_____, *Penjing: Worlds of Wonderment, A Journey Exploring an Ancient Chinese Art and Its History, Cultural Background, and Aesthetics*. Athens, Georgia: Venus Communications, Inc., 1997.

A Note about *The Bonsai Saga*

John Creech wrote about his experiences related to the bonsai coming to America years after the fact. Some details he remembered may conflict with the historical record. His enthusiasm and vision shine through his words, however, and they remain unchanged.

Websites

e360.yale.edu/feature/peter_crane_history_of_ginkgo_earths_oldest_tree/2646/ by Roger Cohn

arboretum.harvard.edu/, The Arnold Arboretum of Harvard University

betterbonsai.com/ by Cheryl Manning

bonsai-nbf.org, National Bonsai Foundation

bonsaipenjing.wordpress.com/ by Hoe Chuah

brusselsbonsai.com/, Brussel's Bonsai Nursery

capitalbonsai.wordpress.com/ by Aarin Packard

fukubonsai.com/ by David Fukumoto

kew.org/, Royal Botanic Gardens, Kew

kofukai.org/, Kofu Bonsai Kai

longwoodgardens.org/, Longwood Gardens

manlungpenjing.org/, Man Lung Penjing

najga.org/, North American Japanese Garden Association

phoenixbonsai.com/, Phoenix Bonsai Society

Shanghai 2010 Expo Official Website

societyofthecincinnati.org/, The Society of the Cincinnati

thehuntington.org/, The Huntington Library, Art Collections and Botanical Gardens

wbff-bonsai.com/, World Bonsai Friendship Federation

Permissions and Photo Credits

The publisher and author thank those who have granted kind permission to reproduce images owned or produced by them, or to include poems or excerpts by them on the pages indicated. Every effort has been made to trace the copyright of all sources and the publisher will be happy to redress any errors or omissions in future editions.

Permissions

22, 23–4, 30–2, 40–2, 88–119, excerpts from *The Bonsai Saga, How the Bicentennial Collection Came to America* by Dr. John L. Creech, by permission of the National Bonsai Foundation.

45 Poem from "A Chinese Garden Court: The Astor Court at The Metropolitan Museum of Art." Metropolitan Museum of Art Bulletin, v. 38 no. 3 (Winter 1980–81). Copyright © 1980 The Metropolitan Museum of Art, New York. Reprinted by permission.

63 John Naka quote from *Timeless Trees* by Mary Holmes Bloomer, Flagstaff, Arizona: Horizons West, 1986, by permission.

63 John Naka proverb from *Even Monkeys Fall Out of Trees* by Nina Shire Ragle, Laguna Beach, California: Nippon Art Forms, 1987, by permission.

86 Eulogy quote from Rev. Marvin Harada, by permission.

Photo Credits

All images courtesy of the U.S. National Arboretum and National Bonsai Foundation unless otherwise noted below, with special thanks to Michael J. Colella and Joe Mullan:

14 (Above) Gift of Mrs. Thomas Powel, Regent and Vice Regent for Rhode Island, and Mr. Powel, 1978; Courtesy Mount Vernon Ladies' Association: W-1612/91.

14 (Above right) Gift of Mrs. E. Crane Chadbourne, Library of Congress: FP2-Chadbourne, no. 8 (A size).

15 Courtesy Hoe Chuah.

17 (Far left) Yokohama Nursery Co. Catalog, 1898, p. 57, and (Left) Yokohama Nursery Co. Catalog 1910, cover; Courtesy U.S. Department of Agriculture, National Agricultural Library, Special Collections.

17 (Below) Courtesy Fairchild Tropical Botanic Garden.

18 (Above left) Library of Congress: LC-J717-X99-2.

18 (Above) Photograph by Louis Buhle, 1915; Courtesy Brooklyn Botanic Garden.

19 (Right) Courtesy JC Raulston Arboretum at NC State University.

21 (Below) Courtesy Richard Nixon Presidential Library and Museum.

31 (Left) Wikimedia Commons.

41 (Below) Freer Gallery of Art, Smithsonian Institution, Washington, D.C.: Gift of Charles Lang Freer, F1903.112.

45 (Below) Courtesy Richard Nixon Presidential Library and Museum.

47 (Above) Freer Gallery of Art, Smithsonian Institution, Washington, D.C.: Transfer from the U.S. Customs Service, Department of the Treasury, F1980.167.

48 (Above left) Freer Gallery of Art, Smithsonian Institution, Washington, D.C.: Purchase, F1975.15.

49 (Right) Freer Gallery of Art, Smithsonian Institution, Washington, D.C.: Purchase, F1957.4.

53 Stephen Voss

57 (photo on left) U.S. Army Corps of Engineers.

59 (Above) Gift of Mrs. Stanley J. Johnson, Scripps College, Claremont, CA: 2000.1.69.

64 (Below right) Courtesy Neil Edmund.

78 (Above) Freer Gallery of Art, Smithsonian Institution, Washington, D.C.: Purchase, 1965.17.

82 (Far right) Stephen Voss

117 Courtesy Peter Bloomer.

121 (Michael James) Stephen Voss

123 Saburo Kato image, courtesy Felix Laughlin.

123 Maria Rivera Vanzant image, courtesy Alan Walker.